KT-178-727

Institute of Biology's
Studies in Biology no. 151

Ageing

Ioan Davies

B.Sc., Ph.D., M.I.Biol.

Research Fellow
University of Manchester
Department of Geriatric Medicine
Geigy Unit for Research on Ageing

Edward Arnold

© I. Davies, 1983

First published 1983
by Edward Arnold (Publishers) Limited
41 Bedford Square, London WC1 3DQ

British Library Cataloguing in Publication Data

Davies, Ioan
   Ageing ⸺ (The Institute of Biology's studies in biology, ISSN 0537-9024; 151)
   1. Ageing   2. Biological chemistry
   I. Title
   612'.67   QP86

   ISBN 0–7131–2863–1

Printed and bound in Great Britain at
The Camelot Press Ltd, Southampton

General Preface to the Series

Because it is no longer possible for one textbook to cover the whole field of biology while remaining sufficiently up to date, the Institute of Biology proposed this series so that teachers and students can learn about significant developments. The enthusiastic acceptance of 'Studies in Biology' shows that the books are providing authoritative views of biological topics.

The features of the series include the attention given to methods, the selected list of books for further reading and, wherever possible, suggestions for practical work.

Readers' comments will be welcomed by the Education Officer of the Institute.

1983   Institute of Biology
                                        41 Queen's Gate
                                        London SW7 5HU

Preface

There is a long history of research into the ageing process and I have attempted to guide the reader from a description of studies on the survival of the whole organism to more recent ones on cellular and molecular ageing.

The subject of ageing has been blighted in the past by the absence of solid data which has led to a literature long on speculation and, until relatively recently, short on fact. I hope I have been able to cast doubt upon certain 'beliefs' about the ageing process.

Ageing is one of the last major problems in biology, and also one of the most neglected. Previous research has largely been confined to the study of whole organism changes such as survival. The recent activity in the fields of cellular and molecular ageing has led to the discovery of new facts about the ageing process, for example, the varietal and species differences in ageing. There is doubt and uncertainty about ageing, which is a characteristic of the study of a 'new subject'.

I would like to acknowledge all those whom I could not cite individually, and to thank all those who helped me by criticising and correcting the manuscript, especially my wife Christine, and my colleagues at Manchester. I want also to acknowledge the support given by Ciba–Geigy Limited to our research unit.

Manchester, 1983   I.D.

Contents

1 Introduction, Ageing, Diseases and *Homo sapiens*

'Do not go gentle into that good night,
old age should burn and rave at close of day;
rage, rage against the dying of the light'

Dylan Thomas (1914–53)

The words of the poet Dylan Thomas reflect the anguish felt by many as they approach the end of life. Throughout history there have been constant attempts to avoid the deterioration of ageing and to postpone death. The search for the 'fountain of youth', or a magical, rejuvenating elixir has ranked highly with the attempts to convert base metals into gold. This metaphysical approach has had a lasting effect on the study of ageing, which until recently was considered by many scientists as a disreputable field for investigation. However, the growth of the elderly population in developed countries has stimulated research into both biological and clinical aspects of the ageing process. This chapter is a general introduction to the biology of ageing and it is oriented towards human ageing since this is the prime concern of man.

The proportion of the population of the United Kingdom over 60 years of age at the present time is approximately 25% women and 18% men. A 60 year old woman has an expectation of life of around 20 years, and a man of the same age one of about 15 years. The majority of these people are compulsorily retired from active working life. Some of the difficulties involved in describing ageing become apparent when we look at the elderly people around us. We all know of 60 year olds whom we consider *old* and 80 year olds who seem relatively *young*. It is also true that the majority of old people are fit and well, but in the less fortunate minority there is an increase in the incidence of diseases and this group consumes a great proportion of the health care budget. Approximately 50% of the hospital beds in the U.K. are occupied by the elderly, and as a group they absorb 25% of all the prescriptions. In addition, the aged usually attend a clinic with more than one disease, unlike younger patients who tend to have only one primary illness. This makes treatment of the old both difficult and costly.

More research into the biological processes of ageing is necessary if we are to treat elderly patients effectively, and so return them to the community to live free of institutional care. Physicians, scientists and others interested in the care of the aged have done much to improve the situation and to convince government planners of the need to provide better facilities for the rehabilitation and care of geriatric patients.

In order to begin scientific research on any topic, it is important to define the problem. Ageing can mean many things. It has social, psychological (behavioural), physiological, morphological, cellular and molecular aspects and a definition encompassing them all does not seem possible. Biologists involved in ageing research operate on the premise that ageing is characterized by a *failure to maintain stability of the internal environment (homeostasis) under conditions of physiological stress*, and that this failure to maintain homeostasis is associated with a decrease in viability and an increase in vulnerability of the individual (COMFORT, 1979). Ageing is obviously a function of time, but development and maturation also involve changes which are age (time)-related. However, both of the last two processes lead to the attainment of peak physiological function, whereas the above definition implies that ageing is a degenerative process. In addition, ageing occurs *after* the period of reproductive activity has ceased. The term *senescence* is usually applied to this part of the life-cycle; it is more precise and is to be preferred when referring to the degenerative effects associated with the passage of time. Plant physiologists however use the term senescence in a somewhat more specialized manner to describe the degenerative and remodelling changes which take place throughout the life-span (see Chapter 2, and WOOLHOUSE, 1978).

The process of ageing is very much a feature of man's life, and it has been argued that it is only expressed because of an artificial protection of the human from its environment. Investigations of animals in their natural habitat have shown that aged animals are rare. Several reasons for this have been put forward, but predation and accidental deaths are probably the major factors involved. The features associated with ageing may not be common in wild animals; but, we know from records kept by zoological institutions that species kept in captivity do show ageing changes and have a longer life expectancy than the same species in the wild. So, what is ageing, and what is its relationship to survival?

1.1   Human survival

Considerable time has been devoted to the analysis of the survival characteristics of human populations. It is no surprise that much of the effort has been made by the mathematicians employed by life-insurance companies! Survival curves for human populations drawn from several different countries are presented (Fig. 1–1).

Inspection of the curve relating to survival in British India in the mid-1920s shows a very high infant mortality, with the 50% survival point being at approximately 20 years of age, and the maximum survival at about 100 years of age. An examination of the survival curve for England and Wales produced from data obtained in the mid-1960s shows a marked contrast to the British India curve and shows a very low infant mortality, and a 50% survival point of approximately 75 years. However, the maximum survival potential is still only about 100 years. Approximately 1 in 10 000 individuals live to the age of 100 years in developed countries, and what is more, there has been no change in the number living beyond 100 years, or in the maximum age at death in the U.K.,

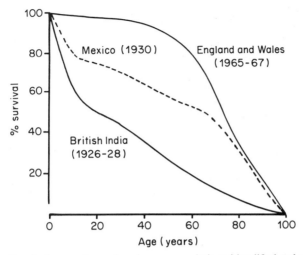

Fig. 1–1 Survival curves for various human populations (simplified and redrawn from COMFORT, 1979).

since accurate recordings began in the nineteenth century. The fact that the median life-span is amenable to such dramatic changes suggests that the major causes of 'premature deaths' in the young age groups have been reduced. The major differences between the two extreme populations discussed above concern their housing, nutrition, public-health facilities (including sanitation) and vaccination programmes. The overall effect of improvements in these variables is to reduce childhood mortality and to increase the numbers of individuals surviving through to middle-and-late-life. Indeed, this is the source of the so-called geriatric problem of today!

Since the maximum life-span potential of man appears to be in the region of 100 years or so, the conclusion drawn is that all of the above mentioned improvements in man's environment have not modified this statistic, and

Table 1 Intra-pair differences in life-span of deceased twin pairs (modified with permission from ROCKSTEIN, 1974).

Age group of first-deceased twin partner	Average within-pair differences in longevity (months)				
	Monozygotic pairs		Dizygotic pairs		
			Same sexed		Opposite sexed
	Female	Male	Female	Male	
60–75 years	47.6	24.0	107.9	88.7	109.7
All pairs over 60 years	47.6	29.4	89.1	61.3	126.6

hence, have not influenced the factors determining maximum survival. This introduces the concept of genetic control over longevity and the idea of a species specific life-span. Other data from life-insurance companies have shown, for example, that the probability of achieving a long life is greater in individuals whose parents have had long life-spans (ROCKSTEIN, 1974). Studies conducted in Scandinavia and the U.S.A. on monozygotic (identical) and dizygotic twins (see Table 1) show clearly that the survival potential of genetically identical twins is very close. However, when genetic variability is introduced the age at death of the first twin pair is no longer a good predictor of the age at death of the second.

In summary, human populations have a recognized survival potential which can be varied with regard to the mean, but so far not the maximum, life-span. This information, combined with the data relating to familial survival characteristics, has led to the concept of genetic involvement in longevity. Since there is genetic control of the processes of development, maturation and longevity, then there is a strong argument for some genetic programme controlling the ageing process itself.

1.2 Physiological effectiveness

Most people measure ageing in terms of altered appearance, declining physical ability and the increase in the incidence of disease. Typical subjective analyses are based on the greying and thinning of the hair, wrinkling of the skin, stooping, and the slowing down and awkwardness of movements. However, personal observation of the elderly in the community shows that such criteria cannot be used to 'age' precisely any one individual. Indeed, it is

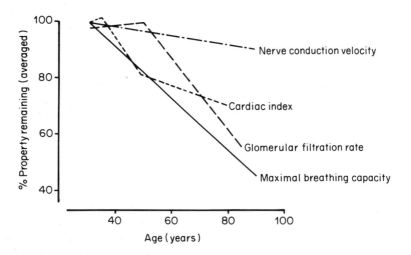

Fig. 1–2 Changes in physiological effectiveness with age (simplified and redrawn with permission from SHOCK, 1956).

plain that chronological and biological age are not the same thing for many people.

Numerous studies have shown a physiological decline with age (Fig. 1–2). The plots of nerve conduction velocity, heart function (cardiac index), maximum breathing capacity and kidney function (glomerular filtration rate) show a considerable decline with age. However, there is usually a high degree of scatter around the mean points for each age group. In fact, a major feature of ageing is an increase in the variation around the mean point for any particular statistic. Caution must be exercised in the interpretation of these data which are derived from *cross-sectional* studies. A cross-sectional study is planned so that a group of one age is compared with a group of another age. One example that illustrates the need for caution is that of *intelligence*. It is frequently stated that as we grow older we become less intelligent. Consider a cross-sectional study using typical IQ testing procedures and attempting to compare elderly individuals of say 80 years, with young people of 20 years of age. The differences between these two age groups, in educational background alone, makes such a study almost impossible without recourse to very specialized testing procedures. Sadly, many investigations have failed to take account of such fundamental problems and many of the sweeping generalizations made concerning the ageing process require re-appraisal.

One way to overcome the defects of cross-sectional studies is to carry out *longitudinal* investigations of a population. In this case the same individuals are observed throughout their life-spans. Such a research programme is extremely difficult to conduct, not least of the problems is that in the case of humans the investigator is ageing at the same rate as his subjects. Preliminary data from such studies reveal age-related reductions in physiological functions but at a less precipitous rate than those shown in Fig. 1–2. Such investigations are of critical importance in the treatment of the aged. For example, a study showing age-related decline in kidney function would indicate caution in the use of drugs metabolized and cleared from the body by kidney tissue.

The longitudinal study also has its drawbacks. The technological advances made in the past 20 years have improved methods of measurement so that our understanding of physiological function has increased correspondingly. This means that longitudinal studies started 30 or 40 years ago often need re-evaluation.

1.3   Ageing and disease

Any discussion of the ageing process would be incomplete without some reference to disease. Many biologists involved in ageing research (gerontology) would argue that ageing changes predispose the elderly to disease. The reduced ability of the aged to maintain homeostasis often leads to serious physiological reactions in response to seemingly minor infections, external temperature fluctuations, or other environmental disturbances. A mathematician, Gompertz, working in the nineteenth century showed that if the logarithm of the species specific death rate (i.e. the logarithm of the number of deaths per 100 000 members of the population) at each age was plotted against age, for deaths from all causes, a linear relationship could be obtained (see Fig. 1–3). If similar plots are made for deaths due to certain specific types of disease then similar relationships may be observed. Such diseases are known as *age-related diseases*. It can be seen (Fig. 1–3) that deaths due to a combination of both malignant and non-malignant tumours (all neoplasia), cardiovascular, renal and cerebrovascular diseases (strokes, *etc.*), parallel the plot for death from all causes. However, there are departures from these relationships, such as deaths due to malignant tumours alone, and diabetes (Fig. 1–3), which do not appear to be the primary killers of the over 70-year-old age group. Infectious diseases (Fig. 1–3) show a very rapid increase in incidence later in the life-span, thus highlighting the problem that the elderly have in coping with infections.

Recent scientific studies of the ageing process have proceeded along welltrodden paths employing model systems drawn from both the animal and plant kingdoms. The following chapters will discuss in more detail, longevity; choice of experimental models; theories of ageing; changes in physiological function; and age-changes in cells and molecules.

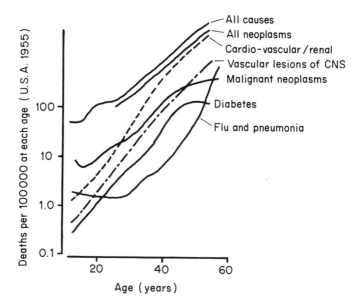

Fig. 1–3 A Gompertz plot of several age-related diseases (derived and simplified with permission from KOHN, 1965).

2 Ageing in Populations and Individuals

In the first chapter we defined ageing, and emphasized the degenerative nature of the process. It is implicit in the definition that the senescent phase of the life-span is characterized by an increased probability of death. The first section of this chapter deals with the evaluation of the survival of populations of organisms through a study of life-table statistics.

2.1 Life-tables

A direct life-table is compiled in the laboratory by studying the survival of a group of animals (known as a *cohort*). The raw data needed are time, and the numbers of surviving animals at that time. The number of survivors (l_x) at the beginning of some specified time interval is recorded, and this can be transformed to a percentage figure to produce a survival curve (Figs. 2–1 and 2–2). The number of deaths noted at the same time is d_x. Other variables can also be determined such as the age-specific death-rate (q_x), and the mean expectation of life (e_x) at each time (COMFORT, 1979). *Populations* said to be *undergoing senescence* show an *increase in the age-specific death-rate* with time. The time scale on the horizontal axis is chosen on the basis of the length of life of the organism; thus in Fig. 2–1, the time for the survival curve for the wasp,

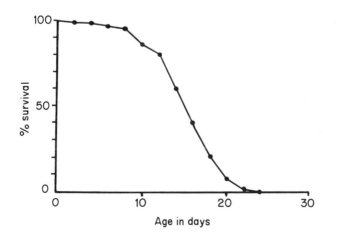

Fig. 2–1 The survival curve for the hymenopteran *Nasonia vitripennis*.

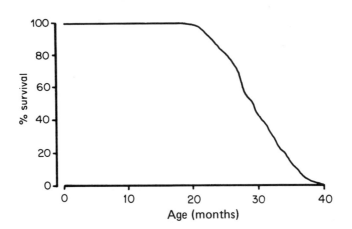

Fig. 2–2 The survival curve for the female C57BL/Icrfa^t mouse.

Nasonia vitripennis, is measured in days and in Fig. 2–2, that for the mouse in months.

The construction of life-tables for natural populations is more difficult. It is possible to determine the age of some organisms by the study of certain anatomical features such as the growth rings found respectively on the shells and scales of certain molluscs and fish, and also in certain trees. In cases where these features can be *linked accurately to a time-scale* then indirect life-tables can be obtained, but they do require considerable care in interpretation (COMFORT, 1979; LAMB, 1977).

In other cases ecologists have devised procedures for constructing direct life-tables for natural populations of birds and fish. Such studies require the 'tagging' of a cohort of young animals (e.g. the 'ringing' or 'banding' of birds), and the periodic sampling of the group to determine the rate of loss of 'tags' from the cohort. There are many obvious problems to overcome in the construction of these life-tables, particularly the loss of 'tags' due to migration and predation. The survival curves produced are usually of the form shown in Fig. 2–3.

In life-tables for such natural populations the age-specific death rate is constant for each time interval and the *population* is defined as not undergoing senescence. However, the small numbers of organisms remaining in the population late in the life-span makes the computation of the age-specific death rate very unreliable. It must be pointed out that the individuals within such a natural population do become senescent (they age), but the life-table does not show the necessary increase in the age-specific death rate with time. If such species are studied in captivity, then invariably the life-table is similar to that found for man, domestic, and laboratory animals. The difference between the two types of survival curve is due to the reduced environmental interactions in the domestic populations.

Life-tables for human populations are of the indirect type, and are

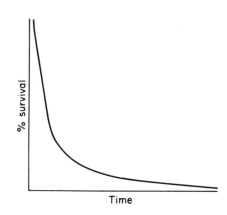

Fig. 2–3   A typical survival curve for natural populations.

constructed using data collected from death certificates and population censuses. Usually the life-table parameters are determined for a *theoretical* cohort of 100 000 individuals using the *age-structure* of the population under study at any given time. Such information is periodically updated so that a form of running commentary can be made on various survival statistics. Figure 2–4 is

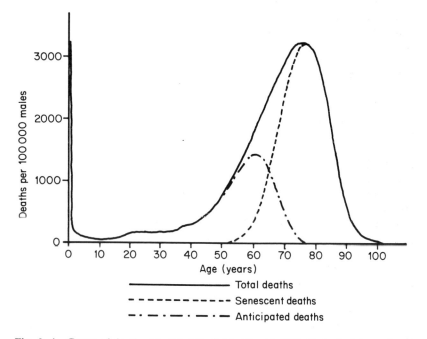

Fig. 2–4   Curve of deaths: English Life-Table No. 11 1950–52 (males) (reproduced with permission from BENJAMIN and OVERTON, 1981).

a 'curve of deaths' which has a major peak at about 75 years for men. The peak occurs at 80 years for women (BENJAMIN and OVERTON, 1981). This terminal peak can be regarded as the central value of deaths caused by senescence. The remainder of the earlier deaths can be attributed to disease or accident. These deaths are known as 'anticipated' or 'premature' deaths, and over the last 130 years there has been a proportional increase in senescent deaths from around 40% of total deaths to over 80% for women, and to more than 70% for men. However, during this period in the U.K. the peak age has only shifted 3 years for men and 9 years for women (BENJAMIN and OVERTON, 1981)!

2.2 Plants

Survival in annual and biennial plants is diagrammatically represented in Fig. 2–5. Typically all the individuals forming a starting cohort will survive for

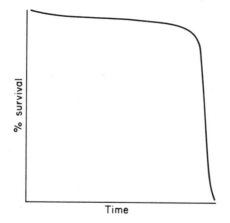

Fig. 2–5   A typical survival curve for the annual plant.

most of the maximum life-span of the species, and then all die. In annual and biennial plants the actual length of life of the plant is linked to flowering and fruiting, after which the entire plant dies. Thus, annual and biennial plants have species specific longevities of one and two years respectively (LEOPOLD, 1978). In the case of perennial plants, notably some of the tree species, the survival times are extremely long. The sequoia (red-wood) trees and the bristle-cone pines can live for as long as 3000 and 4000 years respectively. In these cases the death of the tree is attributed to the mechanical failure of the transport system between the roots and the upper portions of the tree. It must be noted that in these perennial species there is a *continuous process* of *cellular renewal* within a structure which is essentially inert, and it is the cambial layer, found just below the bark of the tree, which is responsible for maintaining life. Thus, this chronologically old support structure is being maintained by a population of cells of unremarkable age.

In plants, therefore, we have very great differences in the length of life between species, from the relatively short-lived annuals with a programme which dictates the death of the complete plant after reproduction has taken place; to the long-lived perennials with life-spans from several to over a thousand years. The event most studied in plants has been the programmed process of growth and degeneration of tissues which the plant physiologists have termed senescence. These events are somewhat similar to the process of development, maturation and cellular renewal in animals which involve similar phenomena of growth and cell death.

2.3   Variation in the length of life

This subject has been exhaustively reviewed by COMFORT (1979). Much of the available information has been obtained from zoo records and in many cases the information must be treated with caution since the maximum longevities reported for some species have been obtained by extrapolation from growth rings and also frequently from body-weight (COMFORT, 1979).

As in the plants we have very great differences in the lengths of life between and within the various animal phyla. Thus, COMFORT (1979) tabulates the maximum longevities for coelenterates as 65–70 years, and for rotifers as about 50 days. Among the Arthropoda we have life-spans ranging from a few days in certain insects to several years in the case of some of the spiders and crustaceans. Molluscs also seem to be capable of living for several years. In the invertebrates the maximum life-spans given usually only relate to the adult stage. Thus, in the insects for example, no account would be taken of the larval and pupal stages prior to the adult phase of the life-cycle. It is possible to obtain over-wintering and diapausing stages in the life-cycle and these can greatly extend the chronological age between the egg and the death of the adult. The influence of environmental factors on natural populations must also be taken into account in the case of poikilotherms, particularly that of temperature.

The reservations expressed above concerning the reliability of the maximum longevity figures determined for invertebrates can be extended to the vertebrates such as fish, amphibia and reptiles. In the case of *natural* fish populations the life-tables suggest that senescence does not take place. In addition, there is strong evidence for continuous growth in many species of fish, presumably because there is no limitation on the maximum size as is found in the land animal. COMFORT (1979) mentions a halibut, about 3 m in length, which was judged by scale examination to be over 60 years old. Bidder hypothesized that the absence of senescence in fish populations was linked to the phenomenon of continuous growth. However, the few studies available on *laboratory-reared* fish show that those species that display continuous growth (such as the female guppy) do become senescent. Studies on the maximum life-spans of reptiles and amphibians are numerous, and, as COMFORT (1979) points out, some of the records relating to tortoises are reliable with ages of over 150 years being documented. Birds are also relatively long-lived (the eagle owl is supposed to live for about 70 years).

There has been considerable interest shown in the variation in the length of life of different mammals. For example, a laboratory mouse can live for about 3 years, the domestic cat for over 30 years and the Indian elephant for 70 years, compared with 100 years, or so, for man. In mammals, but not in other groups, there is a very strong correlation between life-span and body-weight, that is a high body-weight is associated with long life. Alternatively, a low basal metabolic rate is associated with a long life-span. However, man does not fit into this general pattern (SACHER, 1959). Sacher studied the relationship between various body variables and life-span in mammals. A good correlation is obtained with brain weight, but the best relationship of all is obtained when considering both brain and body weight, as the brain:body weight ratio (the so-called *index of cephalization*), in the calculation. Once more caution must be exercised in the interpretation of these data. Although the correlations derived by Sacher and his various co-workers hold in general, they do not always hold in detail. Some mammals which undergo hibernation or overnight quiescent periods, such as the bat, do not conform to the relationship. In this case it is argued that the lowering of the basal metabolic rate during these periods would lead to a longer expectation of life. Also *within* a species there is no close correlation between the various variables mentioned above and life-span. Other factors may also be important and there is a possibility that an increase in brain size may be correlated with a capability to avoid death. Thus, if natural selection favours an increase in brain size, then long life may be a secondary feature of this selection process (LAMB, 1977).

2.4   Immortality, does it exist in animal or plant life-forms?

Not all species undergo ageing. Some of the more primitive eukaryotic cell forms such as the algae, the amoeboid and some of the flagellated and ciliated protozoa appear to undergo division for long periods (probably for ever) unless they are killed by accident. The situation is not simple; there is no clear point of distinction between those protozoa that age and those that do not. Some interesting studies performed by DANIELLI and MUGGLETON (1959) have shown that if *Amoeba proteus* is maintained in culture with a good supply of food then it seems to divide indefinitely. However, the amoebae could be 'spanned', that is a determinite life-span could be induced, by keeping the culture in a maintenance medium which did not support cell division. The conclusion can be drawn, therefore, that the culture conditions play a very important role in determining the mortality or immortality of such species.

In the case of the more complex ciliates such as *Paramecium* however, the processes of either conjugation or autogamy must be completed to ensure the continuation of the colony. Autogamy and conjugation do not normally take place in cultures of *Paramecium* if there are sufficiently good conditions to allow asexual division. However, if asexual division proceeds unchecked then clones of ciliates will age and die out. The only way to avoid the death of a clone is to go through sexual division, and even this process is dependent on clonal age. The conclusion is that these organisms will not divide for ever, and that there is a period of sexual immaturity and maturity in those protozoan clones.

This leads to the question: Is ageing correlated with sexual reproduction? This is very difficult to answer. Certainly some of the algae and protozoa have developed sexual processes but they do not age and die out as long as environmental conditions remain good. It has been stated that 'species can have sex without ageing, but cannot have ageing wihout sex' (SONNEBORN, 1978). Sonneborn concludes that ageing and death evolved later than sexual processes and they were not the 'price paid for sex'.

2.5   The evolution of senescence

Earlier the senescent phase of the life-span was defined as being the post-reproductive decline in viability and survival which accompanies chronological age. Reproduction, and particularly births, are the central components in this evolutionary argument. It has been claimed that natural selection should oppose the senescent decline of an organism. However, it has also been pointed out that natural selection is *least effective* in *manipulating* the characters expressed late in life. The main reason for this (in the context of reproduction) is that the onset of reproductive ability which occurs at different ages has different 'values' in terms of its contribution to future generations. Thus, births taking place early in the life-span of the parent are more likely to be of benefit to the population because the parent has a longer expectation of life and therefore more opportunity to reproduce.

There are four separate proposals that attempt to explain the evolution of senescent processes.

2.5.1   'Age-of-onset modifiers'

MEDAWAR (1952) proposed that certain 'modifier' genes would suppress degenerative, age-accelerating gene effects for as long as possible. Sooner or later however these 'modifier' genes would become ineffective and senescence would take place. Thus, the modifier genes would act beneficially until the organism had achieved full reproductive potential, but it is not clear why these genes would not be selected for and so extend the reproductive period indefinitely, that is, actually defer senescence.

2.5.2   Pleiotropic genes

The concept of pleiotropic genes was invoked by WILLIAMS (1957). He implied that certain genes would be expressed beneficially early in life, but at a later stage in the life-span they would have different, degenerative effects. The period in the life-cycle over which the various effects would be expressed would be determined by the period of maximum reproductive potential.

2.5.3   The allocation of reproductive energy

This theory postulates that genes exist which have the direct effect of shifting the age at which 'energy' for reproduction is expended (GUTHRIE, 1969). In this case senescence would result from the exhaustion of the materials or 'energy' (a poorly-defined term) needed for reproduction and various life-maintenance processes. Referring back to the argument for the beneficial effects of early births, then senescence would be the by-product of a pattern of energy expenditure with a positive adaptive value – the early birth.

2.5.4   Genetic loading

EDNEY and GILL (1968), and later SOKAL (1970), suggested that ageing was the result of the expression, late in the life-span, of accumulated unfavourable mutations and recombinations. The degenerative effects of such a genetic load would have minimum impact on the early fitness of the organism, but would lead to inefficiency and a decline in function late in the life-span.

There have been no exhaustive tests of these proposals. MERTZ (1975) designed an experiment to test whether or not ageing was due to 'age of onset' modifier or pleiotropic genes in the flour-beetle *Tribolium castaneum*. He showed that it was possible to select for improved reproductive performance during early adult life and also to induce higher mortality and lower fecundity in mid- and later-life by such selection. Mertz noted however, that these mortality changes were *independent* of the selection pressures for early fecundity in this insect. He concluded therefore that these observations were not consistent with the phenomenon of pleiotropy put forward by Williams.

ROSE and CHARLESWORTH (1980) also set out to study the evolutionary theories outlined above. The egg-laying performance of female Drosophila was studied at different ages as a way of testing the mutation-accumulation theory (this incorporates both Medawar's and Edney and Gill's hypotheses). They reasoned that the daily egg-laying rate was an easily measured 'fitness component' of reproductive function. Under constant environmental conditions, and if there were no accumulated mutation effects or other deleterious genetic damage, then the insects' egg-laying performance should be constant. However, if effects from either of these proposed sources were present then there would be an increase in the variation of the egg-laying performance with time. No increase in genetic variation could be detected with age and the authors concluded that their data did not fit the 'mutation-accumulation' theory.

To test the pleiotropy theory Rose and Charlesworth selected for increased reproductive output late in the life-span and predicted a decrease in the fertility of the resulting young females and a real increase in life-span. Their results agreed with the predictions of the pleiotropy theory. These authors concluded that senescence in *Drosophila* was due to the late-acting, deleterious effects of genes favoured by natural selection because of their beneficial effects early in the life-span.

So, there is disagreement among the investigators in this field of ageing research. Mertz, using the beetle *Tribolium*, argues against pleiotropic effects, while Rose and Charlesworth, using *Drosophila*, conclude that pleiotropy explains their observations. The disagreement may be due to differences between the insect orders studied, and only more experimental data will help to clarify the situation.

2.6   Ageing within the individual

This section introduces the subject of cellular and tissue ageing within multicellular molecular organisms.

In plants whichever type we investigate there will always be certain processes leading to growth, and others directed towards the death and removal of certain structures such as the leaves and floral parts, these processes are termed senescence by plant physiologists. The development of the seedling is accompanied by cellular death, and similar processes also occur in the fully matured, reproductively active, flowering plant (e.g. the loss of leaves during growth is a precise sequence of events controlled by hormones). In the case of annual or biennial plants the entire organism dies after the flowering and fruiting phase, whereas perennials can continue to function for many years.

In animals development and maturation are accompanied by periodic and selective cell death. In addition, throughout the life-span there is a continuous replacement of cells which are no longer operating effectively in many tissues. Thus, there are fixed life-spans for red blood cells, white blood cells, and cells from the epithelia of the skin and gut. Typically stem cells undergo division and a daughter-cell differentiates into a mature cell, for example, a gut epithelial or a red blood cell. Cells in this rapidly dividing category undergo a process which is dictated by a genetic programme. There are some signs of age-changes in such cells, which are manifested by an increased time interval between cell divisions. However, more obvious age-changes can be seen in cells which either turn-over relatively slowly (e.g. liver cells), or remain as fixed, post-mitotic cells, which are present throughout the life of the organism (e.g. neurones and striated-muscle cells).

How do we distinguish between the processes of development and maturation, and of ageing? STREHLER (1962) set out four criteria that could be used to distinguish between the two sets of processes:

(*i*)   Ageing is *universal*, that is it takes place in all members of the population.

(*ii*)   Ageing is *progressive*, it is a continuous process that takes place in small incremental stages.

(*iii*) Ageing is *intrinsic* to the organism.

(*iv*) Ageing is *degenerative*.

Only the final criterion can be used to separate ageing from age-related maturational processes. In a study of ageing within the individual we are concerned with degenerative change. In fixed post-mitotic or slowly-dividing cells the changes become apparent in any morphological, physiological or biochemical characteristics; while in the study of stem-cell populations we are not necessarily interested in the programme of cell maturation and death, but in the influence of age upon the control and dynamics of this process.

3 Study of the Ageing Process – Models and Methods

In the first chapter we discussed the problems of studying age changes in human populations. Two principal types of investigation were mentioned: cross-sectional and longitudinal studies, each of which had some drawback. Faced with such difficulties it is usual to employ a model system such as another animal, or even to use tissue culture methods. The literature on ageing contains references to studies on protozoans, rotifers, nematodes, crustaceans, insects, molluscs, fish and various mammals.

3.1 Invertebrate animals

The protozoa have been studied in some detail with particular emphasis on clonal ageing and the genetics of the ageing process. Much of the experimental ageing research on invertebrate animals has been perfomed on the rotifers, nematodes and insects. These animals are easy to maintain in controlled, laboratory conditions and have certain advantages in terms of their short life-span and their cellular composition. Each of the individuals in these groups is almost entirely composed of fixed, post-mitotic cells, and since they do not have a well developed cardio-vascular system, these animals provide a unique opportunity to study age-changes in such cells in the absence of alterations to the blood supply.

3.2 Vertebrates

Mammals The ageing laboratory rodent displays many of the features of the ageing process. Fundamental investigations of the physiology, immunology, endocrinology and biochemistry of ageing have been carried out on rats and mice, and constant reference will be made to these during the next few chapters.

A major problem for the gerontologist is which species and strain of animal to choose for study. There are at least 200 inbred strains of mice, each with its own specific life-span and disease patterns. Good animal care is absolutely essential. Adequate records must be kept of environmental conditions, growth rates, food consumption and causes of death. The old animals are particularly vulnerable to respiratory disorders and they must be continuously monitored for possible infections, so frequent bacteriological and viral screening of the colony is required, and routine autopsies are necessary. There is a specific need in some types of immunological investigation for animals to be specified pathogen free, or even maintained in high-security 'barrier' conditions, and free of bacteria, mycoplasma and viral agents. These requirements make the use of laboratory animals in ageing research an extremely complex and *costly* process.

3.3   Tissue culture and *in vitro* ageing

In the early part of the century it was believed that if cells were isolated from a multicellular organism (a metazoan) they would be immortal. Carrel (see CRISTOFALO and STANULIS, 1978), used chick embryo tissues and maintained cultures of the heart cells for over 30 years. Later work on cell cultures derived from normal mouse tissues and human tumours (e.g. HeLa cervical tumour cells), confirmed these early experiments. However, in the early 1960s HAYFLICK and MOOREHEAD (1961) described a different situation when they showed that cells from a variety of normal human tissues would only proliferate in culture for a specific period before degenerating and dying out. Cells such as these were clearly not immortal and the suggestion was made that this was the cellular expression of the ageing process.

Culture procedures   Human cell cultures are obtained from pieces of fresh tissue (*explants* from either embryonic sources, or small skin biopsies from adults). These explants are incubated in a sterile nutritive medium and cells migrate out from the sample and form a layer within the culture flask. The medium resembles blood serum, and for cells to grow and divide it must contain a certain proportion of animal or human serum. The cultured cells are elongated and spindle-shaped, and are defined as human diploid, fibroblast-like cells. Fibroblasts are commonly located in connective tissues and are responsible for the synthesis of collagen.

The cells attach to the surface of the culture flask and divide rapidly. Eventually a 'mat' of cells forms which completely covers the surface of the medium. The cells then stop multiplying (mediated by a process known as 'contact inhibition'), and will usually only divide again when stimulated in some way, usually during the process of *sub-cultivation*, also known as *passaging* the cells. The cells are released from the flask by enzyme treatment, re-suspended in fresh medium, divided, and placed into two new culture flasks. The cells divide again and once the contents of a flask have divided and filled the two vessels the *culture* is said to have undergone a *doubling*.

This process of sub-cultivation can be carried out many times. The *accumulated population doublings* are used as a measure of the culture age (Fig. 3–1). The cells display different growth characteristics at different stages of the culture life-cycle. In the early stages the cells proliferate rapidly and the sub-cultivation intervals are short. Eventually the cells become larger in size, and are much slower to divide, this is the *senescent phase* of the culture. The average number of population doublings of foetal lung and skin fibroblasts before the senescent phase is approximately 50, and the average total number of doublings is 63.

If cells are isolated from adult humans, as compared to foetal sources, there is a reduction in the number of population doublings that can be achieved by the cells. Thus, instead of a potential of 50 doublings, only 30 can be obtained

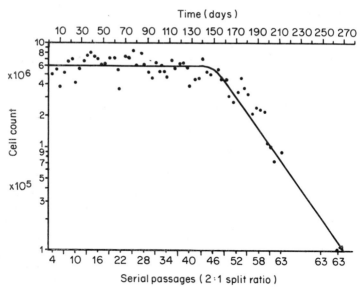

Fig. 3–1 Cell yield during ageing in a human diploid cell culture (reproduced with permission from HAYFLICK, 1965).

before the senescent phase. This system of sub-culture allows the freezing and storage of large quantities of material at defined 'age groupings'.

There are species differences in the response of fibroblast-like cells to culture conditions. Chick fibroblast-like cells have a stable, limited life-span and never appear to give rise to 'immortal' cell lines. Similar cells from mice and rats also have a characteristic growth pattern which comprises rapid proliferation of the cells followed by a decline, and then almost always a spontaneous transformation into an immortal cell line. Human cells on the other hand can be 'transformed' to an immortal cell type by some treatment, such as exposure to a virus (e.g. Simian virus 40, CRISTOFALO and STANULIS, 1978).

To return briefly to Carrel's original experiment, nobody has been able to repeat his work and no-one knows why. One possible explanation is that live chick cells were introduced into his experimental cultures when fresh embryo extract was added to feed the cells. Other immortal cell lines are now known to be abnormal and 'malignant' in type. Indeed many of the cells were derived from tumour tissue, and were capable of forming tumours if transplanted into laboratory animals. In addition, there are distinct nuclear differences between 'malignant' and diploid, fibroblast-like cells, both in terms of chromosome number and/or morphology (CRISTOFALO and STANULIS, 1978).

The *in vitro* cell system can be used in the experimental approach to many fundamental questions concerning the ageing process.

3.3.1 Cell physiology

Various biochemical and physiological studies have been made, such as investigations of the DNA content and DNA repair mechanisms of senescent cells. While the DNA content remains constant with age there is a reduction in the efficiency of DNA repair in old cells but the exact mechanism of this change is unclear. Studies of the levels of RNA and protein in senescent cultures show that, in general, there is an increase in content, but a decrease in the rate of synthesis of both components implying an alteration in turnover rates. Morphological changes seen in senescent cells include increases in cell size, a decrease in the nuclear-cytoplasmic ratio and an increase in ageing pigment.

3.3.2 Cell division kinetics

Senescent cells in culture have a reduced proliferative capacity. If young cells in culture are labelled with radio-active DNA precursors then there is a uniform incorporation of the label suggesting that most of the cells are undergoing division. In old cultures only a small percentage of the cells are labelled (approximately 20%). In addition, cells from old cultures have a longer inter-division time and it appears that many senescent cells are 'arrested' in the pre-DNA synthesizing phase of the cell cycle.

The population doubling time is the critical factor in the determination of a cell's age. Cultures can be frozen at a particular doubling stage and later thawed, the re-cultured cells then continue to divide until they achieve the average number of doublings characteristic for their strain at that age. Cells can also be 'maintained' without division for prolonged periods by reducing the amount of serum in the culture, and then, simply by adding fresh serum they continue dividing for the normal number of divisions for the strain.

3.3.3 Accelerated ageing in humans

There are genetic syndromes which have relevance to the pathobiology of human ageing. Several of the so-called *progeroid* (accelerated ageing) syndromes have been proposed as models of ageing in humans, and furthermore, fibroblasts isolated from such individuals have been used to study certain age-associated changes in functional ability.

There are three classical progeroid syndromes; Hutchinson–Gilford, Werner's, and Cockayne's syndromes (MARTIN, 1978). These conditions are characterized by young individuals having a senile appearance. In the Hutchinson–Gilford syndrome this is manifested in the facial features, but in the more severe Cockayne's form there is a senile appearance combined with dwarfism, mental retardation, degeneration of the eyes, and deafness. Each of these syndromes is autosomal recessive in its mode of inheritance.

Fibroblasts from patients with these abnormalities have a shorter *in vitro* life-span than fibroblasts from normal adults of the same age. Fibroblasts isolated from Hutchinson–Gilford and Werner's patients only undergo 10 doublings as compared to the average of 30 doublings in cells derived from normal adults. There have also been reports of decreases in mitotic activity,

DNA synthesis, DNA repair efficiency and cloning efficiency in cells isolated from individuals with these syndromes. It has been claimed that the study of fibroblasts from these subjects will give valuable insights into these conditions and may also prove to be a starting point for the genetic analysis of the ageing process in humans.

One other condition, Down's syndrome, shows certain features of accelerated ageing (MARTIN, 1978). Down's syndrome is commonly referred to as mongolism, and is a condition of mental retardation with various associated abnormalities caused by the presence of three copies of chromosome 21 (trisomy). There are variations of the trisomy which arise as a result of non-disjunction (failure of the pairs of the chromosomes to separate during mitosis). The abnormalities associated with these conditions are many and until relatively recently such individuals were not expected to live beyond about 20 years of age. However, improvements in medical care mean that these individuals can now live at least 40 years. Brain autopsy specimens from these patients have been shown to have the neuropathological signs associated with senile dementia. This is a very important finding and it is possible that examination of Down's syndrome subjects will give important clues as to the genetic factors predisposing towards senile dementia, perhaps through a study of isolated fibroblast-like cells.

3.4.   Methods of studying ageing

There are essentially two ways of studying the ageing process. Firstly, one can study the feature of interest at various stages of the life-span, and secondly, one can manipulate the life-span by using techniques to shorten or extend it.

3.4.1   Study of particular age-stages

The method of study can be either cross-sectional or longitudinal. We have already discussed the difficulties of studies of these kinds in human populations where we are faced with widely different genetic backgrounds, exposure to disease and environmental stresses. Most animal studies involve research on genetically defined, highly inbred strains of animals, or crosses between such strains, so in carefully conducted experiments animal variation is not usually the major problem. Much of the remainder of the book will describe the results of such investigations so the subsequent discussion in this chapter will be devoted to experiments attempting to manipulate the life-span.

3.4.2   Life-span manipulation

It has been said that the only way to study the ageing process is to manipulate it. Various techniques have been used to shorten life-span, such as exposure to ionizing radiation. Some early studies, mainly based on histopathological changes, suggested that exposure to radiation led to accelerated ageing and this topic will be discussed further in Chapter 4 (see somatic mutation theory). Increasing oxygen concentrations and high temperatures can also be used to shorten the life-span under certain conditions (see Chapter 4, free-radical theory of ageing). The relevance of life-shortening effects to the study of the ageing process has been questioned. Unless the agent used causes the uniform acceleration of age-related events it is not acceptable; however, it is difficult to see how this criterion can be rigorously applied since it is impossible to measure all spects of the ageing process simultaneously. It seems that we are on much safer ground if we extend the life-span.

Life-span extension has been attempted using several approaches. Certain drugs such as β-aminopropionitrile (BAPN), and anti-oxidants such as vitamin E, are claimed to extend the life-span and these observations will be dealt with in Chapter 4 (sections on the cross-linkage and free-radical theories of ageing respectively). The hormone hydrocortisone can extend the number of population doublings of fibroblast-like cells in culture, but only if it is present throughout the life-span of the culture. It is not effective if applied only in the senescent phase of the life-span.

There are two reliable methods of extending the life-span of experimental animals. In poikilothermic (cold-blooded) animals, either a reduction of temperature or dietary manipulation have been shown to extend both the mean and maximum life-spans. In homeotherms (warm-blooded), dietary manipulation is the only method successful in extending life-span.

Temperature reduction Several eminent biologists at the turn of the century argued that life-span was related to the metabolic rate of the organism, and in the case of the poikilotherms this could be manipulated by alterations in temperature. The theory proposed was termed the *rate of living* theory. Many interesting experiments were performed, and in general high temperatures shortened life-span and low temperatures extended it.

However, one study complicates the issue. When *Drosophila subobscura* adults were transferred from a temperature of 20°C to 26°C they lived the same length of time as flies maintained at 26°C for their complete life-time. CLARKE and MAYNARD-SMITH (1963) argued that if ageing was temperature dependent then the flies should have lived longer than those kept permanently at 26°C. It was proposed that there were two stages to the life-cycle: a temperature independent ageing-, and a temperature-dependent dying-, phase. This is the *threshold theory of ageing* and it was proposed that a balance existed beween the production and consumption of essential cellular constituents (loosely termed 'vitality'), the use of which was related to the metabolic rate of the insect. Young flies were able to maintain the balance between production and use of 'vitality', even at high temperatures, but as they grew older this balance could only be maintained at lower temperatures.

These experiments have been criticized by SOHAL (1981) who pointed out that it was assumed that temperature influenced the metabolic rate in a directly proportional manner but this was not confirmed by measurement. Subsequent studies have investigated the effects of both temperature and metabolic rate on life-span. For example, the 'shaker' mutant of *D. melanogaster* has nervous system defects and the animals are abnormally active. The metabolic rate of the mutant is higher than for normal *D. melanogaster* and the length of life of the 'shaker' is proportional to its metabolic rate. Other experiments have shown that ambient temperature, physical activity and ageing are closely interrelated in the house-fly *Musca domestica*. The life-span of the house-fly is inversely proportional to physical activity, and the effect of temperature on the life-span is very much dependent on the temperature-associated variation in physical activity (SOHAL, 1981).

Dietary manipulation   It is possible to extend the life-span of all animals so far investigated by manipulation of the diet, usually by restricting the food intake. The early experiments on the crustacean *Daphnia* showed that life-span increased if food was restricted, and later experiments by McKay and his co-workers showed that the same effect could be demonstrated in mammals also.

The effect of *calorie* restriction, that is, the provision of a fully balanced diet *complete* in *all aspects of nutritional requirement*, but *reduced in quantity*, allows the animal to attain a very significant increase in life-span. Indeed, increases in the order of 100% in maximum life-span have been obtained under certain circumstances. The effect of dietary restriction is reproducible and is effective in both rats and mice. Invariably the reproductive development of the animal is delayed. Rats which have been maintained on a restricted diet for long periods, in some cases longer than the mean life-span previously recorded for the species, can be re-fed on an *ad libitum* diet, and in these circumstances growth resumes and they live out a much longer life-span.

There are beneficial side-effects to this life extension; one is that the onset of age-related diseases is significantly delayed in restricted animals, another is that the restricted animals appear 'fitter' than normally fed rats. The development of the immune system is also delayed. Studies on enzyme activities in dietary restricted animals show that they differ from both normal control animals of the same age, and fully-fed rats of a much younger age. Thus, we do not appear to be studying a *slowing down* of the ageing process, rather that dietary restriction launches the animal on a completely different developmental pathway.

Some of the recent work, particularly that from Ross's laboratory in the U.S.A. (ROSS *et al.*, 1976), has shown that the longevity of rats can be predicted surprisingly accurately (even when they are allowed freedom of dietary choice), solely on the basis of their dietary behaviour and growth responses early in life. In these experiments three diets, with the same calorific value, but differing in their protein:carbohydrate ratios (10:75%; 22:55%; and 51:29.5% protein:carbohydrate respectively) were presented simultaneously to individual rats and records were kept of the intake of each individual diet. Each rat selected a diet differing in both quantity and composition. In general dietary composition did not correlate as well with life-span as did body-weight variables. Animals that chose, and efficiently utilized, a low-protein (but otherwise complete) diet early in life, and also completed the greater part of their growth by 100 days of age, would probably be *short-lived*. Conversely, rats that grew slowly, particularly between 50 and 150 days of age would be more likely to *live longer*. Calorie intake was not an important factor influencing the ageing rate of the rats in this experiment, but according to the authors this was not necessarily at variance with earlier work. They point out the importance of the interactions between rate of growth and body weight in the determination of subsequent events. Thus, the variables such as absolute body weight changes, and the times required to attain specific weights are very important, and these seem to be related to the protein : carbohydrate ratio in the diet early in life.

Much more work is necessary using this model for the manipulation of the life-span of laboratory animals before an accurate assessment can be made regarding the influence diet has on both ageing and survival. Proposals have been made suggesting that dietary restriction alters some fundamental 'clock' mechanism, while others have put forward the idea of a so-called dietary hypophysectomy (removal or inactivation of the pituitary gland). The two ideas are connected in that the hypothalamus of the brain is central to the control of all physiological functions, and mediates much of this activity by means of the pituitary gland. COMFORT (1979) has suggested that the hypothalamus contains a 'clock' mechanism which could control the ageing process, but there are insufficient experimental data available to be able to assess such a hypothesis critically. An alternative view can be put forward regarding the effect of diet on life-span. The unlimited intake of food (*ad libitum* feeding) by rats and mice in captivity was probably adopted so that maximum growth could be obtained. It could be that maximum growth rate is not (as Ross's work implies) conducive to the attainment of maximum longevity, and that the *ad libitum* diet actually shortens life-span.

4 Theories about Ageing

The earliest theories about ageing were invariably associated with the reduction in sexual activity observed in men of advanced age, and it was suggested that the overall cause of ageing was a reduction in gonadal function. It was subsequently proposed that ageing could be delayed, and the life-span increased, if 'gonadal preparations' were taken by old males. Chronic exposure to bacterial toxins was also implicated as a cause of ageing, and certain types of food were advocated to reduce such effects. However, treatments of this kind have failed to modify the ageing process in humans. The theories about ageing have mainly been of a·speculative nature; they are not usually based on experimental observations, and, since these are rather difficult to obtain, the theories have been incorporated into the literature of the subject. I have confined the discussion in this section to the major theories, but it will become painfully clear that there is not a great deal of experimental support for most of them (SCHOFIELD and DAVIES, 1978).

There are broadly two alternative views on the cause of ageing. Firstly, that it is the result of some *programmed, time-dependent degeneration* of the organism, and secondly, that it is the result of *random damage* to *cellular structures* which leads eventually to tissue disorganization.

4.1 Programmed ageing

We have already seen from the study of life-table statistics that there are characteristic species specific life-spans. It is partly from such findings that the idea of a genetic influence on the life-span has been formulated. Much of these data have been assembled from studies of inbred (brother–sister mated for many generations) strains of animals. Inbred animals are homozygous for many characters and are more genetically uniform than outbred stocks. Each inbred line has its own characteristic length of life which is generally shorter than the species specific life-span. This is known as 'inbreeding depression'. Two such inbred lines can be crossed and the first generation (F_1) hybrid so derived invariably has a longer life-span than the parent stocks (COMFORT, 1979). This increase in life-span, along with other improvements, is termed 'hybrid vigour' or *heterosis*. Thus, genotype can affect the length of life of a particular strain, but, there have been no systematic studies of the differences in the expression of the rate of ageing in animals of different genotype.

Another important feature of ageing is the more or less consistent finding that females live longer than males. However, from the studies so far no correlation has been found between longevity and the different types of genes associated with the X-chromosome in humans. It is clear from studies on animals that which sex will live longer can be dependent on the particular strain. The situation is further complicated because we know that sexual activity can influence life-span in females. Thus, in both the mouse and *Drosophila*, there is evidence for a shorter life-span in mated as compared to virgin females.

Several genetic mechanisms have been proposed to account for ageing phenomena, and they are intimately connected with ideas concerning the evolution of the ageing process. This topic has been dealt with in Chapter 3. The hypotheses referred to require much more extensive testing before they are accepted or rejected. The following discussion concerns other genetic mechanisms which have been invoked to explain ageing.

4.1.1   The codon-restriction theory of development and ageing

Strehler and his colleagues (references in SCHOFIELD and DAVIES, 1978) proposed the codon-restriction theory of development and ageing. They saw the life-span as a continuum of change from development, through maturation to ageing, with each 'stage' being determined by its predecessor. The theory states that ageing is due to the degeneration of various long-lived components which are formed during early development. In the process of differentiation the synthesis of these long-lived materials is repressed.

Differentiation involves cellular specialization which usually limits the types of protein synthesized by the cell. This limitation in the types of proteins produced is determined by the genes available for translation at any given time. These genes are termed the cell-type specific codon sets. In a complex metazoan the various genes of the cells are 'turned-on' (de-repressed), or 'turned-off' (repressed), so that suitable proteins are produced at the appropriate time. One cannot exclude the possibility that during this process some genes (which previously coded for essential proteins), would be repressed but they could still be essential for the continued functioning of the cell after differentiation had ceased. Any accidental event which leads to the damage or loss of cell components, whose particular proteins are coded by these now repressed codon sets, could be expected to lead to the death of the cell.

As a test of this hypothesis the genes available for transcription at any given time in the life-cycle can be characterized by changes in the specific types of transfer RNA (tRNA), and other components of the protein synthetic apparatus (such as the tRNA synthetases). Changes in the complements of such molecules have been recorded during developmental processes, cell differentiation and hormone stimulation, but not with ageing.

4.1.2   Gene redundancy

There is considerable repetition of DNA nucleotide sequences (genes) in the genome of eukaryotic organisms. The presence of this so-called *redundant DNA* is thought to be a reserve of evolution, and a method for increasing the functional expression of genetic information. However, it may also serve as a way of protecting these genes from any random molecular damage that may take place. Medvedev, and later Cutler, proposed that multiple copies of essential genes could be a protective mechanism for the conservation of information, and may play a role in the *determination of the ageing rate* for a particular species. Cutler determined the overall percentage of redundant DNA coding for ribosomal RNA (rRNA), but failed to find any correlation between this and the ageing rate (based on the maximum life-span potential). However, it has been shown that a large number of the genes coding for messenger RNA (mRNA) are to some degree redundant in mammals with a potentially long life-span.

The evidence for protection of the genome by means of redundant DNA is poor. Medvedev's prediction that a large increase in redundant DNA leads to a great increase in species longevity is not supported by Cutler's work.

4.1.3   Gene dosage

Various investigators have studied the hypothesis that the numbers of genes coding for ribosomal RNA (rRNA) available for transcription at any time, the gene dosage, might be correlated with longevity. The rRNA gene dosage has been found to vary in certain species at different stages of the life-cycle. However, estimations of the numbers of rRNA genes that can be transcribed late in the life-span as compared to early on have been inconclusive. In mice the

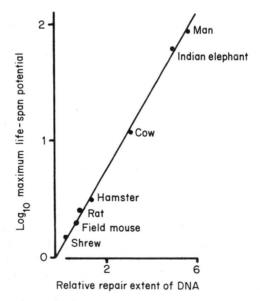

Fig. 4–1 The correlation between the efficiency of DNA repair and the maximum life-span potential of several mammalian species (modified with permission from HART and SETLOW, 1974).

rRNA gene dosage was lower in the liver than in the brain of young animals, but after 12 months of age the liver rRNA gene dosage increased to the levels found in brain. No differences in rRNA gene dosage in either the liver or the brain, in connection with either sex or age could be detected in humans.

4.1.4   DNA repair mechanisms

Efficient DNA repair would be one strategy whereby an organism could maintain the integrity of the genome for long periods. It has been suggested that animals with a long life-span potential have a more efficient DNA repair system. Evidence for this has been obtained from studies on fibroblast cultures exposed to high doses of ultra-violet (UV) radiation. Both the initial rate and the maximum incorporation of radio-actively labelled DNA precursors into DNA increased with the life-span potential of the species as shown in Fig. 4–1.

4.2   Unprogrammed ageing

4.2.1   Waste product theory

The cells of most ageing organisms show increased levels of pigmentation. These pigments (termed lipofuscin) are particularly prominent in the fixed, post-mitotic cells of the heart and the brain.

Lipofuscin is an irregular granular inclusion within cells (Fig. 4–2). This pigment can emit a yellow-green to orange fluorescence when excited by UV-light. The lipofuscin granule is extremely heterogeneous, it contains proteins, carbohydrates and lipids, and various enzymes associated with lysosomal activity and oxidative metabolism. In the electron microscope lipofuscin is highly irregular in shape and there is a certain variation in structure which is dependent on the cell type (Fig. 4–3).

There have been several hypotheses put forward concerning the intracellular origin of this material; the main organelles implicated have been the mitochondria, endoplasmic reticulum and the lysosomes but there is now general agreement that lipofuscin is associated with the process of intracellular autophagy. This topic has been reviewed recently (SOHAL, 1981).

Lipofuscin is found in greater quantity in the cells from old animals. Some studies claim that up to 30% of the cell volume is taken up by the granules. Studies on post-mortem brain tissue from old humans have demonstrated that neurons are packed with lipofuscin which some have suggested may influence cell function by lowering the levels of RNA within these cells.

There is now some evidence however, for the turnover of this material. A study of the neuroendocrine cells responsible for the production of the peptide hormones vasopressin and oxytocin shows that in old mice approximately 2% of the intracellular volume is occupied by lipofuscin, as compared to 1% in the cells from young ones. However, under conditions of osmotic challenge (when there is a massive release of vasopressin from the posterior pituitary and the initiation of hormone synthesis in the neuroendocrine cells) there is also a reduction in the volume of lipofuscin in the cells. Re-hydration leads to a progressive increase in the volume of lipofuscin in these cells back to the levels

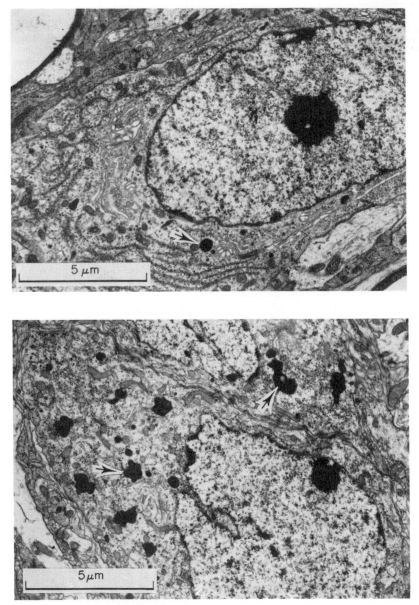

Fig. 4–2 Low magnification electron micrographs demonstrating the increase of lipofuscin in neuroendocrine cells of the ageing animal. The upper micrograph was taken from a 6-month-old male mouse and the lower from a 28-month-old mouse (courtesy of A. P. Fotheringham).

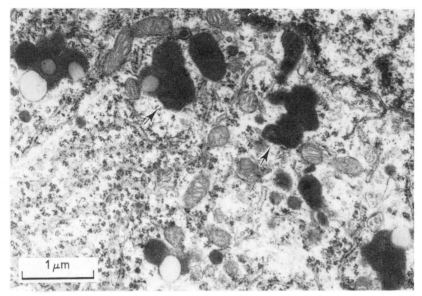

Fig. 4–3 The variation in the structure of lipofuscin in a neuroendocrine cell from a 28-month-old mouse (courtesy of A. P. Fotheringham).

seen in old control animals. The implication is that lipofuscin undergoes some form of turnover, in other words it does not necessarily accumulate with age, it is merely found in higher concentration in the cells of older animals (DAVIES and FOTHERINGHAM, 1981). Several workers in this field of research now suggest that lipofuscin is an *indication* of cell damage with age, and that it probably reflects an increase in the rate of cellular autophagy, perhaps due to damage caused by free-radical reactions (see section 4.2.3) (SOHAL, 1981). It is clear from this discussion that we know very little about lipofuscin or its effect on cell function.

4.2.2   Cross-linkage theory

The abnormal cross-linkage of macromolecules has long been regarded as a cause of the ageing process. In the 1950s cross-linkage of the connective tissue proteins collagen and elastin was considered the major factor in the ageing process, but this theory has now been extended to cover the cross-linkage of strands of DNA and DNA-protein within the chromosome.

Collagen and elastin   The structure of collagen and elastin is well understood. The bulk of the published work centres on the assembly and stabilization of the collagen and elastin fibres during the development and maturation of tissues, rather than the age-changes. The cross-linkage of collagen or elastin molecules is essential for their correct functioning, however, age-changes are thought to be due to *excessive* or *abnormal* cross-links, other than those required for mature structural efficiency.

Age changes within connective tissue proteins have been detected as alterations in their physical properties (e.g. reduced tensile strength, extensibility, elasticity and compressibility) but it is also claimed that in the case of basement membranes there may be also a reduction in their permeability to nutrients and waste-products.

Indirect, physico-chemical measurements have been used in the search for increased collagen cross-linkage with age and these will be discussed in Chapter 6. More direct, chemical and enzymatic dissection techniques suggest marked changes in the nature and extent of cross-links in human tendon collagen between adulthood and old age. Complete characterization of these cross-links is still awaited however, and in recent years more attention has been paid to the idea of qualitative, post-maturational changes in the collagen cross-links increasing the stability of the molecular structure.

It is known that the cross-linkage of collagen and elastin is inhibited by compounds known as lathyrogens (e.g. β-aminopropionitrile, BAPN). The administration of these drugs modifies the cross-linkage pattern, and if this has a significant beneficial effect on the ageing rate of the organism, it should cause an extension of the life-span. The results from experiments of this kind have been contradictory. Some authors fail to find any effect on the life-span of rats and mice after feeding these compounds, while others note that the mean life-span is increased by approximately 10%.

The fact that the mean life-span can be modified by these drug treatments implies that some age-related pathological process is being affected rather than some fundmental, intrinsic ageing process. Further work will be needed to assess the significance of these results, especially since some of the studies suggest that some form of dietary restriction is also taking place in the treated animals.

DNA and chromatin   There is experimental evidence for the presence of inter-strand cross-links in the DNA from bacteria, insects, and cultured mammalian fibroblast-like cells, however, their role in the ageing process is uncertain. Direct estimates of inter-strand cross-links in *Drosophila* reveal that betweeen 6% and 9% of the DNA is cross-linked in this way, and that this level does not alter with age.

Several investigations of chromatin-template activity show age-related reductions in function. Typically the isolated DNA-protein complexes display a reduced template activity towards DNA-dependent RNA polymerases. However, if the DNA is purified from the DNA–protein complex then the age-related changes in activity can be abolished. It is proposed that these changes are due to interactions between the chromatin sub-units, although their exact nature is unknown.

Whatever the interactions are within the chromatin structure, they are not irreversible. Simple *in vitro* procedures can reverse these changes, but whether or not this is also true *in vivo* is unknown. There have been claims that free-radical reactions could cause these supposed cross-links, so presumably the inhibition of such reactions could have beneficial effects on cell function. These findings are extremely important, since it seems clear that ageing in animals is to some extent governed by alterations in gene expression.

4.2.3 Free-radical theory

Free-radicals are formed by the splitting of a covalent bond in a molecule so that each atom joined by the bond retains an electron from the shared pair. These reactions are common in normal cell physiology. HARMAN (1956) proposed that *uncontrolled* free-radical reactions could be an important source of cellular damage in a variety of pathological processes, and that they could initiate ageing. Free-radical damage was thought to take place throughout the life-span causing a progressive deterioration of both nuclear and cytoplasmic components.

The free-radical hypothesis is linked to the idea of *oxygen toxicity*. The respiring organism is in a difficult dilemma, it respires and obtains energy from the action of oxygen, but oxygen itself can be extremely toxic; to overcome these problems several defence mechanisms have been evolved to protect the organism. HALLIWELL (1981) discusses the phenomenon of oxygen toxicity in a recent review.

Free-radicals Most of the oxygen in an aerobic organism is reduced to water by the cytochrome oxidase enzyme complex of the inner mitochondrial membrane. However, some oxidases within the cell can generate hydrogen peroxide which is extremely toxic, and in the presence of transition metal ions such as iron, can decompose to form the hydroxyl radical $^{.}OH$.

$$Fe^{2+} + H_2O_2 = {}^{.}OH + Fe^{3+} + H_2O$$

Other enzymes catalyse oxidation reactions in which a single electron is transferred from a substrate onto each oxygen molecule, this produces the oxygen free-radical known as the superoxide.

$$O_2 + e^- = O_2^{.}$$

This radical is a by-product of various enzyme reactions, (particularly in the mitochondrial and chloroplast electron transport systems), and can also be caused by environmental agents such as UV-light, ultrasound, X- and gamma-rays, toxic chemicals and metal ions.

Free-radicals can cause lipid peroxidation. Membrane lipids usually contain numbers of poly-unsaturated fatty-acid side chains. These fatty-acids undergo lipid peroxidation which involves the generation of carbon radicals and finally lipid hydroperoxides. These lipid hydroperoxides decompose to aldehydes (e.g. malondialdehyde) and other products, which are cytotoxic, causing damage to both enzymes and membranes. These various radicals react with and damage all molecules found within cells, and the lipid and protein components of membranes seem especially vulnerable. In addition, DNA can be altered causing 'strand-breaks' and mutations.

Protection against free-radicals   Protection of the cell against free-radical damage is effected by several mechanisms. For example, glutathione is a tripeptide which contains 'free' sulphydryl groups, and is thought to protect against the toxic effects of oxygen:

$$2GSH + \frac{1}{2}O_2 = GSSG + H_2O \tag{1}$$
$$GSSG + NADPH + H^+ = 2GSH + NADP^+ \tag{2}$$

where, GSH is glutathione
GSSG is reduced glutathione
and reaction 2 is catalysed by glutathione reductase.

Hydrogen peroxide on the other hand can be removed by two types of enzymes, the catalases and the peroxidases. Another enzyme, superoxide dismutase, acts specifically in the removal of the superoxide radical:

$$O_2^{\cdot -} + O_2^{\cdot -} + 2H^+ = H_2O_2 + O_2$$

'Scavenging' systems are also present to protect the cell from lipid peroxides. For example, vitamin E (α-tocopherol) is incorporated into the membrane structure and is thought to trap free-radicals.

There are age-related changes in these protective systems. Thus, there is less glutathione and glutathione reductase in the red blood cells of older mice, and there are age-related defects in the superoxide dismutase from the livers and brains of old animals.

As a test of the toxic effects of oxygen it has been shown that an increase in the oxygen:nitrogen ratio in the ambient air shortens the life-span of *Drosophila*, and leads to an increase in the concentration of lipofuscin. However, attempts to extend animal survival by feeding anti-oxidants such as vitamin E through the life-span have been inconclusive. There is usually a beneficial effect of 10–15% on the mean life-span depending on the strain of animal, but the maximum life-span remains static. These experiments are difficult to interpret because the treatments result in a decrease in body-weight, so that these animals may be restricting their food intake, which can in itself lead to extension of life. In spite of these reservations we have to accept that anti-oxidants can influence the life-span of some species. In addition, the feeding of anti-oxidants has been shown to reduce the levels of fluorescent pigments in mouse tissues. Conversely, diets inadequate in vitamin E generally result in accelerating the deposition of lipofuscin in both the nervous system and the adrenal glands of rats and mice. Hence the intracellular appearance of lipofuscin may be associated with free-radical damage within cells.

The impressive list of potentially damaging free-radicals suggests that they may be instrumental in causing serious damage to cells, and this may predispose the cell to ageing changes. However, the effects of anti-oxidant supplements in the diet are equivocal and more direct evidence is required before accepting that free-radicals do have a central role in the cause of ageing.

4.2.4   Somatic mutation theory

It has been proposed that mutations in somatic cells will cause changes in function. Two scientists, Failla and Szilard (see references in SCHOFIELD and DAVIES, 1978), independently proposed that somatic mutations were the cause of ageing. Failla, assumed that *dominant* mutations were the cause of cell damage or death. Szilard, on the other hand, considered that ageing in diploid cells was due to *recessive* mutational events, and if one of a pair of homologous genes is damaged or 'hit' and subsequently inactivated, the other member of the pair would continue normal functioning, whereas, if both of the homologous genes were damaged, either through a previous 'hit' or some hereditary fault, then both members of the pair would be inactive and cell damage would ensue. In either case, eventually large numbers of cells would become inefficient and the organism would die.

Both versions of this theory have been severely criticized. One prediction from both is that inbred organisms should live longer than outbred ones, the reason being as follows. The inbred is homozygous at most loci, whereas outbreds are heterozygous at many positions. Inbred organisms cannot be homozygous for genetic defects because this is often a lethal combination. Since the inbreds will be heterozygous for very few 'faults' then it follows that they will express close to the species-specific life-span. However, all the evidence obtained on inbreeding effects points to a reduced life-span.

Szilard's theory also predicts that in species with both haploid and diploid individuals the diploid organisms should have a longer life-span than the haploid ones, and that the haploids should be more susceptible to life-shortening effects such as ionizing radiation. Studies on the wasp *Habrobracon* have shown that such predictions are not fulfilled. The female wasps are diploid, but the males can be obtained with both haploid and diploid gene complements. The haploid males have the same life-span as their diploid counterparts, which is inconsistent with the theory, but, they are more susceptible to the effects of ionizing radiation.

The results of several studies on the life-shortening effects of ionizing radiation, have been claimed as evidence in support of the somatic mutation theory of ageing. Laboratory rodents die as a result of exposure to ionizing radiation with the appearance of both malignant and non-malignant causes of death earlier in the life-span. This has been described as accelerated ageing. These findings are disputed on the grounds that the types of pathological changes generated are not identical to those seen in ageing. The situation is not made any simpler by the fact that different doses of radiation affect survival in different ways. Thus, low level radiation can increase the life-span of some insects and mice, but high levels of radiation usually shorten it. At certain dosage levels the irradiation of old animals is less effective at shortening the life-span, and in some very old age-groups there is an increase in life expectancy. The explanation for this seems to lie in the removal of potentially malignant, actively dividing cells in the older age groups.

Some connection has been claimed between events of somatic mutation and the presence of chromosomal aberrations in ageing cells (CURTIS, 1971). The aberrations consist of chromosomal bridges and fragments which can be seen in dividing cells. In long-lived strains of mouse the aberrations increase from an incidence of approximately 10% in 2-month-old animals to about 35% in 24-month-old mice. In short-lived mice they develop much more rapidly, from 20% at 2 months to 80% at 20 months. Strains with intermediate life-spans have an intermediate rate of accumulation of aberrations.

However, there are also exceptions to this finding. Some mice with very short life-spans have a rate of accumulation of aberrations which is similar to that found in mice with long life-spans. This is probably because these animals develop severe pathological lesions, such as leukaemia or mammary carcinoma, and hence are not ageing in the strict sense of the term. Perhaps a more serious difficulty is that F_1 hybrids derived from parents with different life-spans develop chromosomal aberrations at a rate intermediate between that of the parents but actually live significantly longer.

These observations are difficult to interpret. It is not clear that radiation produces the same form of mutation as maybe associated with the ageing process. In the case of chromosomal aberrations we have no evidence that they are overt signs of somatic mutation, and/or there is a functional consequence due to their presence. It is not clear that chromosomal aberrations are harmful to survival, and one of the more potent tests of the hypothesis, the F_1 hybrid study, is not convincing. Thus, we have little experimental evidence available to support or refute the somatic mutation theory. Nevertheless, somatic mutation has been claimed as a 'trigger-event' for age-related changes in the immune system (see Chapter 5).

4.2.5   Errors in protein synthesis

This is one of the more recent theories of ageing. It was proposed by ORGEL in 1963 and modified in 1970. He argued that there was a small, but finite possiblility that errors could take place in protein synthesis. He suggested that incorrect amino-acid insertions into proteins could take place with age, but that the actual error frequency was uncertain. His preliminary estimates were that a possible low value would be 3 in 10^8 correct insertions, and that a high one would be 1 in 10^4 insertions. Incorrect amino-acid insertions could have various effects depending on where they occurred within a protein. If the 'errors' were at the catalytically active site of the enzyme for example, this could alter its activity, or its specificity for a substrate.

In many proteins these changes may have little effect, for example in the case of proteins undergoing rapid turnover. However, errors in the enzymes involved in the processing of genetic information (the various DNA and RNA polymerases) could be potentially more damaging. These polymerases have relatively long half-lives and catalyse a large number of reactions before they are degraded. Any alteration in their function could lead to the introduction of a large number of error-containing proteins which would accumulate within the cell. Orgel suggested that a critical level of such proteins in the cell could occur, and this would be followed by an 'error catastrophe' and cell death.

This theory was seized upon by many biochemists and a period of intense activity followed as experiments were conducted to detect 'error-containing' proteins. Technically this is very difficult to do since it is impossible to detect the error frequencies proposed using conventional techniques. Indirect approaches have therefore been employed and these will be discussed very briefly.

Heat-labile proteins Many experiments have been conducted on the assumption that the thermal inactivation kinetics of an enzyme will be altered if it contains errors. It had previously been shown that mutant proteins, containing specific amino-acid replacements, were abnormally sensitive to heat. The findings of experiments such as these will be discussed in Chapter 6, but for the purposes of this section the results so far have been somewhat contradictory.

Viruses as probes of inaccurate protein synthesis One rather ingenious and elegant test of Orgel's hypothesis utilized viruses as probes. These experiments were performed in the *in vitro* human diploid, fibroblast system and tested the ability of the protein synthesizing machinery of these cells to support viral growth. In a virus infection the protein synthesizing machinery of the host cell is used to make new viral protein. If senescent cells contain a transcription and translation apparatus that is prone to errors then this should result in a reduction in the numbers of viruses produced, or abnormalities in the viral proteins. This in turn may make the assembly of the new viral particle less efficient and changes such as these could alter the infectivity of the new virus. However, senescent cell cultures supported infections by three different viruses as well as young cultures, and the yields of new virus were equal in each case. The infectivity of the viruses was also identical, and in addition, there was no evidence of an increased mutation rate.

Protein turnover studies Some investigators have studied the rates of turnover of proteins as a test of the error hypothesis. The rationale for studies of this kind is based on the observation that abnormal proteins are turned over at increased rates when compared with normal proteins. Freshly isolated liver tissue, from animals of different ages, shows no age-related increase in the rate of protein synthesis. However, studies on tissue culture systems suggest that proteins produced by *terminal* senescent cultures have an increased susceptibility to proteolytic degradation. The conclusion drawn has been that if this increased degradation is due to mistranslation, then it is an effect of *in vitro* senescence rather than a cause of it.

There is now doubt as to whether or not errors in protein synthesis are a primary cause of ageing. The various indirect methods used have given contradictory results, and indeed, there are alternative ways of interpreting the data. One factor consistently ignored by many of the investigators is the possibility of *post-synthetic* modifications in protein structure (SHARMA and ROTHSTEIN, 1980), and these will be discussed in Chapter 6.

4.2.6 Generalized error theory

The uncertainty and contradiction generated in tests of the various theories put forward has led to the formulation of a generalized error theory. It will be shown in Chapter 6 that there is a potential for multiple molecular damage to take place during ageing in molecules of diverse types ranging from nucleic acids to proteins.

It must be emphasized that there is no single theory about ageing that explains all the known facts concerning the ageing process. From the above discussion it is clear that none of the proposed mechanisms of ageing can be completely excluded. Thus, although some of the evolutionary and genetic mechanisms may be instrumental in determining the maximum life-span potential, and to a certain extent the ageing rate, the various unprogrammed events (which may be partially modulated by external circumstances), can also play a significant role.

5 The Physiology of Ageing

All investigations so far have shown a reduction in physiological efficiency with age, and in this chapter we will review aspects of age-related alterations in the reproductive physiology of laboratory rodents, humans and plants. This will be followed by a description of age-changes in the endocrine and immune systems.

5.1 Reproductive ability

Every animal species shows an impairment in reproductive ability with age. There is a considerable variation in how this decline in efficiency is expressed which is dependent on both the sex and the species involved. Studies of the reproductive potential of the metazoa can be divided into several areas; the physical ability of the adult to undergo sexual reproduction, the viability of the germ cells, the sex of the animal, and also endocrine factors.

5.1.1 Reproductive behaviour

It has been shown that there is a change in mating behaviour with age. In male animals there is a reduced ability to undergo mating, and there is an alteration in the receptiveness of the ageing female to the mating male. The male rat shows a reduction in explorative and locomotor behaviour with age and this has been correlated with altered mating behaviour.

Among insects a study of *D. melanogaster* males showed that peak 'mating performance' was maintained over the first four weeks of life, when mated with females approximately one week old. 'Mating performance' was measured by recording the latency period before a male mated with a female, the number of matings per given time period, the duration of copulation and the number of progeny resulting from each mating. From four weeks of age to the end of the life-span (approximately seven weeks), the 'mating performance' of the male decreased. In females of different ages mated to young males there was a reduction in the tendency to undergo mating with an increase in age.

Sexual behaviour is extremely complex and to understand the process the endocrine status of the animal must be known. For example, the receptivity of the old female mammal depends very much on the stage of the oestrus cycle reached by the animal under investigation. The hormones controlling reproduction are produced by the hypothalamus and the anterior pituitary and are diagrammatically represented in Fig. 5–1.

5.1.2 Reproductive hormones – age changes

Many studies have been directed to determining whether or not there is a

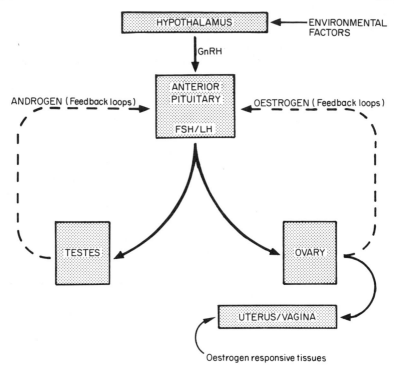

Fig. 5–1 The regulation of the secretion of sex hormones.

primary age-related failure of the hypothalamic-anterior pituitary axis or the ovary.

Females After about 18 months the laboratory rodent ceases to display the regular 4- to 5-day changes in the oestrus cycle, and in older rats and mice phases of constant oestrus and pseudo-pregnancy are common. An old female, in the state of constant oestrus, shows no cyclic surges of the gonadotrophic(GnRH)-, luteinizing(LH)-, and follicle stimulating (FSH) hormones, prolactin, oestrogens or progesterone. Serum prolactin, however, is increased in old rats and is believed to be partly responsible for the increased incidence of spontaneous mammary cancer in some of these animals. In addition, even under conditions of appropriate stimulation, the old, irregularly cycling rats, show a reduced capacity to release LH and FSH from the anterior pituitary. In the ageing laboratory rodent however, the ovaries remain potentially functional throughout the life-span.

Of major importance in the regulation of the hormonal surges in the oestrus cycle are changes in the levels of hypothalamic neurotransmitter molecules. These neurotransmitters are involved in passing information to and from the various brain regions, and age-changes in these pathways may lead to disturbances in the oestrus cycle. There are reduced levels of the hypothalamic catecholamines (noradrenalin, adrenalin and dopamine), and an increase in serotonin (5-hydroxytryptamine), in old as compared with young rats. These catecholamines (particularly noradrenalin), stimulate GnRH release whereas serotonin inhibits it. In addition, dopamine inhibits, and serotonin stimulates prolactin release. The decline in hypothalamic catecholamine levels, and the rise in serotonin levels, in old rats may account for their reduced capacity to secrete GnRH and may also be responsible for the increase in serum prolactin.

In women the menstrual cycle fails at around 50 years of age. For several years prior to the *menopause* the menstrual cycles tend to become irregular and shortened. There are pronounced ovarian changes during this period, the number of cycles when ovulation does not take place is increased, and some pathological events such as the development of cysts are more frequent. In the post-menopausal period the ova and follicles remaining in the ovaries degenerate, as does the ovary itself.

In the period prior to the menopause there is a reduction in the secretion of hormones by the ovaries and in the post-menopausal phase there is an almost total lack of these hormones in the serum. However, the secretion of the gonadotrophic hormones from the anterior pituitary rises rapidly in an apparent attempt to stimulate the ovaries. These hormone levels remain high for many years after the menopause.

Males   No age-related reduction in the levels of the anterior pituitary hormones can be detected in healthy male mice. If GnRH is used to stimulate the anterior pituitary to produce LH then no age-related effects can be detected. Thus, in some strains of mice certain responses to trophic hormones by both the pituitary and the testes are maintained throughout life, whereas in certain strains of rat (Wistar and Long-Evans) an age-related impairment does exist (FINCH *et al*, 1977). These findings imply species differences in the effect of age on pituitary and testes function in rodents.

In humans there has been much talk of a male 'menopause' but its physiological basis is uncertain. A recent report using *strictly healthy* aged, volunteers shows that serum levels of male sex steroid hormones are not influenced by age even though the serum LH levels rise significantly (HARMAN and TSITOURAS, 1980).

Thus, to summarize, in the ageing female rat the ovaries appear to be capable of normal function to the end of the life-span, and the cause of the disruption of the oestrus cycle lies in the age-related changes seen in the hypothalamic- anterior pituitary axis. In the ageing human female we have the converse situation with primary failure of the ovaries.

On the other hand ageing males (both rodent and human) tend to show a more gradual decline in reproductive function, and a major factor in this process could be the influence of age-related pathologies in both the laboratory rodent (NELSON *et al.*, 1975) and in man.

5.1.3 Viability of germ cells

In insects there is a reduction in fecundity through the life-span. It has also been shown in other studies that the progeny from older parents are more likely to be defective in some way (containing chromosomal aberrations, etc.), or to have a shorter life-span. LANSING (1959), reported that the eggs from old parthenogenetic (i.e. reproduction by an ameiotic division of the egg-yielding clones of genetically identical offspring) rotifers, produced offspring with a shorter life-span than eggs from young rotifers. This was in spite of the fact that the offspring had identical genotypes. A clone propagated from old rotifers always died out because the longevity of each succeeding generation became shorter. The clones from old rotifers could be rejuvinated by breeding through young parents, indicating that the effect was reversible, but those clones derived from young rotifers had a constant life-span. Lansing suggested that some cytoplasmic factor had an unfavourable effect on longevity.

Evidence for a maternal age effect has been recorded in mice and an age-related increase in the frequency of foetuses with chromosomal abnormalities has been found. In humans the maternal age-effect is correlated with an increased frequency of offspring with chromosomal abnormalities. The most common disorder is Down's syndrome (see Chapter 2). It has been shown that a 20-year-old mother has a probability of 1 in 2300 of having a Down's baby as compared with a chance of 1 in 40 for a woman at the age of 45 years. The reason for an increase in the frequency of chromosomal abnormalities in the offspring of older mothers is unknown. Several hypotheses have been put forward, ranging from the result of the normal ageing of the egg and/or the female reproductive system, to the cumulative exposure of the female to agents capable of inducing chromosomal abnormalities.

5.2 The reproductive system of plants

As stated previously the term senescence is used in a somewhat more specialized manner by plant physiologists. There are five groups of hormones implicated in the senescent changes that take place in plants; the *auxins*, *gibberellins*, *cytokinins*, *abscissic acid* (ABA) and *ethylene*. Each of these hormones has specialized functions within the plant; the auxins (for example, indolylacetic acid, IAA) and the gibberellins are involved in the regulation of cell size; the cytokinins regulate cell division; ethylene can influence cell shape, and ABA controls the process of abscission or shedding of redundant parts of the plant (WOOLHOUSE, 1978).

In the plants that produce flowers and fruits only once before they die (monocarpic plants), the life-span can be extended by the removal of the flowers as soon as they form. The physiological mechanism for this is unknown (WOOLHOUSE, 1978). It was suggested at one time that these plants died after flowering because essential metabolites were diverted to the developing seeds. However, this hypothesis has now been abandoned in favour of other mechanisms which range from an irreversible shut-down of the growth of the root systems to the possible generation of lethal signals produced by the developing seeds.

The process of senescence in the reproductive components of plants has been reviewed by WOOLHOUSE (1978). Flower-petal cells lose RNA and soluble proteins during senescence, and in the later stages there is an increase in the activity of hydrolytic enzymes. These changes are of considerable importance to the 'cut-flower' industry and a great deal of research has centred on the process of senescence in flowers isolated from the plant. Senescence can be delayed by treatment with cytokinins and accelerated by ABA. These changes can be complicated, however, if leaves are left attached to the stem. In this case ABA causes a closure of the leaf stomata, which reduces water losses and delays petal cell senescence. On the other hand, cytokinins can delay leaf senescence, increase water losses and accelerate petal senescence.

Senescence at the fruiting stage is also of considerable economic importance. Fruits can be either fleshy or dry in consistency, and in both cases there is a regulated process of senescence which leads to the development ('ripening') of the final product. 'Ripening' includes diverse events such as colour changes, the production of soluble sugars and other organic molecules, and also the 'softening' that takes place in fleshy fruits.

The hormone ethylene has been attributed a major role in the ripening process. However, according to WOOLHOUSE (1978), it is difficult to unravel the various sequences of events associated with the softening of the fleshy tissues. The early stages of fruit development are regulated by hormones produced in the seeds. Each of the plant hormones can be found during this process and it is apparent that the relative proportions of the different hormones control the development and translocation of materials to the fruit itself. Nevertheless, the hormonal changes that are critical in the ripening process are still unknown. In some fruits, such as tomatoes, a delay in the ripening process has been correlated with high levels of cytokinins and this is reminiscent of the situation described above for the 'cut-flower' system.

The senescence of the reproductive processes in plants is dependent on sequential changes in hormonal activity which is somewhat similar to the situation in animals. However, in both animals and plants the molecular events leading to these changes are not yet characterized except that concentrations of hormonal molecules in tissues are altered.

5.3   Age-related endocrinological changes

The study of age-related changes in the endocrine system has been gathering momentum in the last decade. The working hypothesis has been that ageing is similar to development and maturation in that it is an endocrine-mediated process.

The endocrine system is complex but there are five components basic to its mode of action:

The endocrine system is complex but there are five components basic to its mode of action: (*i*) The *detection* of changes in the external or internal environment by a *receptor* system. (*ii*) The stimulation of the *production or release* of hormone in response. (*iii*) The transport of the hormone to some *target tissue*, which may be another endocrine gland, or some other organ. (*iv*) The *response* of the target tissue to the hormone, and the return of the internal environment to a *steady-state* (homeostasis). (*v*) *Feed-back* to return hormone secretion to the steady-state.

Depending on which part of the endocrine system is being studied the sensory input could be either chemical or synaptic. The input of chemical information into a cell is mediated by receptor systems, and the type of receptor depends on the chemical nature of the stimulating hormone. The cells of the neuroendocrine system also have synaptic contact with various regions of the central nervous system.

On receiving a stimulus the endocrine cell can either synthesize the hormone or release it immediately if it is stored in sufficient quantity. In most cases the hormone is then transported in the peripheral blood to a target tissue where chemical receptors mediate the action of the hormone. The initiation of the target tissue response follows a well-described route. Various feed-back mechanisms then take place to limit the production of hormone as necessary.

5.3.1 Age-related changes in endocrine cell response

Several studies have been directed to the levels of receptors in endocrine cells. The Leydig cells of the testes of rats respond to increased levels of gonadotrophic hormones by the synthesis and secretion of testosterone, but no age-related changes in this system have been detected *in vivo*. Conversely, under culture conditions, Leydig cells show a marked reduction in testosterone secretion after incubation with gonadotrophic hormone. Although the Leydig cells isolated from old rats show a 27% reduction in gonadotrophic receptors the total intracellular cyclic adenosine monophosphate (cAMP) generated is not significantly different from that of cells from mature animals. These findings suggest that some intrinsic, intracellular defect occurs which limits the production of testosterone by isolated Leydig cells, and that these defects, although associated with a reduction in gonadotrophic receptors, are not necessarily related to defects in cAMP production.

The response of the endocrine cell to physiological stress can be followed by studying the changes induced in cellular morphology. A study of the vasopressin- and oxytocin-producing cells in the hypothalamus of the mouse showed no age-related changes in the production of hormone containing organelles. In addition, under conditions of osmotic stress, where these cells have to synthesize fresh hormone, hormone granule production did not decline with age (DAVIES and FOTHERINGHAM, 1981a).

5.3.2 Age-changes in the levels of circulating hormone

The serum levels of hormones have been used to study the secretory capacity of endocrine organs, but an age-dependent decline in hormone production is difficult to detect. When hormone levels are correlated with lean body-mass, no decline is found corresponding to the decline in lean body-mass of old humans. The hormone levels tend to remain constant throughout the life-span (GUSSECK, 1974).

Thyroid hormones have been implicated in the regulation of enzyme levels in tissues, the permeability of cell membranes, protein synthesis and metabolic rate, but there is no overall age-related decline in hormone production. Yet, there is a decrease in the utilization of these hormones by body tissues. The function of the adrenal glands as indicated by the basal plasma cortisol levels show no consistent alteration with age. Knowledge of the steady-state level of hormone in blood though, is not always useful in interpreting the effect of age on the rate of hormone production or tissue utilization. In the case of most endocrine glands there appears to be a considerable reserve capacity even in the old animal.

5.3.3   Target-tissue responsiveness

If a physiological stress is imposed on an ageing animal, there is usually a delay in the appearance of the response. This has been amply demonstrated in studies on enzyme induction in response to a cold stress or to other, more direct forms of endocrine challenge. It has been shown that ageing animals can undergo a delay of from several minutes to several hours in these induction processes (Fig. 5–2).

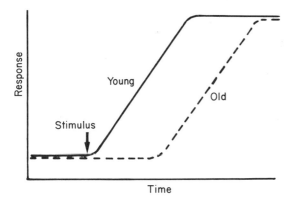

Fig. 5-2 Age-related delay in the induction of enzymes. A typical graph showing that the rate of induction and peak responses are similar, but that the initial response is delayed.

Several studies have shown a reduction in target-tissue endocrine receptors with age. One model system used has been the post-mitotic fat-cell (adipocyte). The numbers of receptors for noradrenalin on adipocytes of the *same size* are reduced, so that the cells from rats at 8 months of age have approximately 41 000 receptors, while at 30 months the numbers of receptors fall to approximately 7000. Decreases in receptor numbers for neuro-transmitters, peptide and steroid hormones have been observed in diverse tissues including brain, skeletal muscle, liver and gonads, and in cells such as lymphocytes and human-diploid, fibroblast-like cells (ROTH, 1978).

ROTH (1978) also points out that age-related receptor loss is not universal. Losses have been detected in some tissues during development and maturation, but not during adult-hood and ageing. In addition, an increase in certain types of receptor has been shown in both the seminal vesicles and skin fibroblasts.

These changes are difficult to analyse, partly owing to different techniques generating different results, such as in tissue culture when actively-dividing cells are compared with non-dividing cells. Another puzzling problem is that of different changes that occur in the same receptor type. Thus, there is no age-related change in noradrenalin receptors in the cerebral cortex, but there are significant reductions in these receptors in the cerebellum and the corpus striatum of the brain.

Another problem of interpretation lies in the complexity of tissue structure. This is frequently ignored in biochemical investigations. There are numbers of different cell types within a tissue, thus, in brain we have several neuronal types, several glial populations, the neuroendocrine cells and those cells associated with the blood-vascular system and the ventricular ependymal cells. In this context the term 'brain cell' has little meaning. A detailed study should be made of *defined* cell populations at various stages of the life-cycle, but this is technically very difficult to do.

5.4   Ageing of the immune system

The immune system plays a critical role in the defence mechanism against invading micro-organisms and toxic compounds and in the removal of cells which have 'escaped' from normal function and which may transform into tumour tissue.

It has been proposed that ageing could be due to changes in the immune system. WALFORD (1969) suggested that ageing is due to somatic cell variations, particularly of those factors which determine self-recognition among cells, and is brought about by the unleashing of self-destroying processes of the nature of autoimmunity or transplantation disease. This has been put forward as the immuno-pathological theory of ageing. The cells of the immune system would be 'altered' by either somatic mutation or some other genetic lesion. Thus, it is possible that post-mitotic cells with long life-spans might acquire different antigenic properties with age thereby inducing the immune system to attack and destroy them. Alternatively, as a result of genetic damage, the lymphoid cells may become more, rather than less, tolerant with age and so fail to destroy aberrant cells, such as cancer cells. In fact, there are age-related increases in the incidence of neoplasia, infections and autoimmune diseases (Chapter 1).

5.4.1   *Immune system components*

The immune system is comprised of various organs including the thymus, spleen, various lymph nodes (such as the tonsils), and the bone marrow. The cells of the immune system are the lymphocytes (T- and B-cells) and the macrophages.

The various cell types in the immune system act together to form an *immuno-competent unit*. The macrophages are extemely versatile in function and participate in the immune response in different ways. Their central role is to concentrate antigens and present them to the lymphocytes. In addition, the macrophages secrete biologically-active mediators capable of regulating the type and magnitude of the lymphocyte reaction, either by enhancing or suppressing cell division and/or differentiation. These activities are in addition to the role of the macrophage as a phagocytic cell involved in the removal of dead cells and bacteria.

The lymphocytes are the specific cell components of the immune system. The T-lymphocytes (thymus-derived, T-cells) fall into two functional categories, the regulatory and the effector cell types. The regulatory T-cells can either help ('helper') or suppress ('suppressor') the responses of other T- or B-cells. The effector T-cells are responsible for cell-mediated immune reactions such as the rejection of foreign tissue grafts and tumours (the graft versus host reaction), and the removal of virus-infected cells. Both the graft versus host reaction and the killing of virus-infected cells requires the participation of T-lymphocytes known as 'killer' cells. The B-cells synthesize and secrete all the classes of the antibody protein immunoglobulin which is one of the most important molecular products of the immune system. The antibody proteins are produced in response to stimulation by an antigen. There are several immunoglobulin classes, designated as immunoglobulin A (IgA), IgD, IgE, or IgM, each with different functions. Most of these molecules circulate in the plasma and they operate at a distance from the site of production. In addition, the immunoglobulin molecules also serve as antigen-specific receptors on the surface of the B-lymphocytes.

5.4.2   Age-related changes in the immune system

Age-related changes take place in the lymphoid tissues with the most marked alterations occurring in the thymus. The thymus reaches its maximum weight early in life and thereafter there is a rapid regression of the tissue. The maximum weight of other lymphoid tissues is usually reached early on in the life-span and then stays stable or declines very slowly with age.

It is well known that the rate and the magnitude of the immune response is subject to a variety of cell regulatory controls. Any study of the mechanism of age-related changes in intercellular regulation is difficult. Usually a particular cell component of the immuno-competent unit is studied in the presence of *optimum numbers* of other cells derived from *young animals*. In such an experimental system it may be difficult to determine whether or not the 'age-changes' so observed are due to the effector cells or the regulatory cells in the mixture. In some experiments, for example, those described in KAY and MAKINODAN (1981) the responses of some 'young-old' cell mixtures were less than some of the responses given by pure 'young' and pure 'old' cell mixtures.

Stem-cell function   A population of pluri-potential stem cells maintain the lymphocyte and macrophage populations. Any stable, intrinsic alteration in these stem cells will affect immune capacity. Transplantation experiments have been conducted to test stem-cell function. In studies of this kind *immuno-logically compatible* (syngeneic) animals must be used, so that there is no graft versus host reaction on the transplantation of tissues between animals. The animal receiving the transplant (host) is exposed to a potentially lethal dose of radiation to remove the stem-cell populations completely. The success of any subsequent transplant is measured in terms of the survival of the irradiated host. Experiments involving transplants will be discussed in Chapter 6. For the purposes of this discussion the ability of the stem cells to divide tends to decrease with age. Attempts have been made to study this deficit by allowing stem cells from old animals to replicate in syngeneic young recipients for a long period. However, subsequent examination of the stem-cells shows that they are not 'rejuvenated'. In addition, stem cells from young donors, when allowed to replicate in old recipients, display the kinetic properties of stem cells *from aged animals*. Thus, stem cells seem to undergo irreversible alterations in the ageing animal, and the nature of the environment of the old animal can influence the kinetics of stem cells from young animals.

Such age-related alterations of the kinetic properties of stem cells could be crucial in disease-stressed old people. As an example, it has been shown that immunologically immature young, and immunologically inadequate old, mice, both develop auto-antibodies against red blood cells following a virus infection. Notably, the young mice with auto-antibodies *do not become anaemic, whereas old mice do*. Thus, when stressed by infection, old individuals may not be able to maintain homeostasis by increasing cell production to compensate for increased cellular destruction. In addition, the observation that stem cells from young animals are required for the complete immuno-restoration of ageing mice supports the view that changes intrinsic to stem cells contribute to age-related immune system defects.

Macrophages   Macrophages are readily isolated from the lining of the abdominal cavity of the mammal (the peritoneum), and neither the number of peritoneal macrophages, nor their antigen-processing ability, nor their phagocytic activities are altered with age. *In vitro* the phagocytic activity of the macrophages from old animals is equal to that of young mice and, also, the activity of the lysosomal enzymes in both splenic and peritoneal macrophages increases with age. More recently the antigen-processing ability of macrophages has been assessed using slightly different techniques. When young and old mice are injected with different doses of sheep red blood cells, it has been shown that the slope of the antigen dose/antibody response curve is lower in old animals, and that the minimum dose of antigen needed to generate a maximum response, is significantly higher.

Lymphocytes–T-cells   A decrease in the number of T-cells in the thymus has been detected in some strains of ageing mice. In humans the number of circulating T-cells has been reported as either decreasing progressively after adulthood or remaining the same throughout life. There is also evidence suggesting that age-related alterations take place in the chromatin of mitogen responsive T-cells which may explain the delays in the initiation of cell division and the decrease in proliferation rate.

There are age-related qualitative changes in the T-lymphocyte. At the cell surface both a loss of receptors and a different type of new receptor are observed. There is also evidence that changes in the properties of the lymphocyte plasma membrane can reduce the responsiveness of T-cells to certain forms of stimulation. Evidence for the emergence of new receptors comes from various sources. Kay has described a *human cell senescence antigen* that is an indicator of cell senescence independent of the age of the individual. The emergence of this antigen on the surface of senescent red blood cells initiates regulatory IgG auto-antibody binding and the removal of the cells. Most importantly, this antigen also appears on the cells of mice bred and maintained in high-security 'barrier' conditions, implying that the senescent cell antigen is expressed independently of any microbial antigens.

Shifts in the sub-populations of T-cells have also been demonstrated. The proportion of certain T-cells which are short-, compared to long-, lived, has been shown to decrease with age in some mice. Suppressor T-cells have been seen both to decrease and to increase in proportion with age. Some studies using short-lived strains of mice, suggest that suppressor T-cell activity declines with age. These data have to be interpreted with caution since the causes of both the decline in normal immune function, and the increase in immuno-deficient diseases in animal models such as these may be quite different from those occurring in long-lived mice. Studies in long-lived mice imply that the relative number of suppressor T-cells tends to increase with age but that 'helper' function declines.

Lymphocytes – B-cells   The number of B-cells in humans and mice does not change appreciably with age. If anything, the number in the spleen and lymph-nodes tends to increase. Although the total number of B-cells remains stable, the relative sizes of certain sub-populations change.

The responsiveness of B-cells to stimulation decreases strikingly with age. Studies in which the responses of young and old mice were systematically evaluated showed that the decline is caused by two factors. One is a decrease with age in the number of antigen-sensitive immuno-competent precursor units which are made up of two or more cell types. The second is a decrease in the average number of antibody-forming functional cells generated by each immuno-competent precursor unit. The reasons for the reduction with age in the relative number of immuno-competent precursor units is unknown at present. Qualitative changes in the B-cells, similar to those seen in T-cells, also take place with age.

This has been a very short summary of some of the knowledge available on age-related changes in immune function. Normal immune functions can begin to decline as early as the period of sexual maturity. The decline is due to both changes in the immune cells and in their environment. Cell loss, shifts in the proportions of sub-populations, and qualitative cellular alterations – the three possible types of change which could cause a decline in function – have all been detected. The major alterations appear to occur in the regulatory networks where the interactions beween cells and molecules required for an *effective immune response* are disrupted.

6 Ageing – Cells and Molecules

6.1 Cellular ageing

Most research in this field has been conducted on mammalian cells. There are four principal cell-types within the body:

(*i*) The fixed, post-mitotic cells such as the neurons and the striated muscle cells.

(*ii*) The cells that remain capable of division throughout the life-span but otherwise turn-over very slowly, such as the cells of the liver, kidney and cartilage.

(*iii*) Cells that divide rapidly throughout the life-span of the organism, but have themselves a relatively short life-span ranging from days to months. The cells in this category are the lymphocytes, red blood, skin, and gut epithelial cells.

(*iv*) Stem cells that maintain the cell population described in (*iii*).

It has been argued that only the cells in categories (*i*) and (*ii*) will show intrinsic ageing changes, since these cells are present throughout the life-span of the organism. This view is not necessarily correct, and indeed we have previously discussed some aspects of age-related changes that take place in the cells of types (*iii*) and (*iv*). Yet, the importance of cells such as the neurons, means that considerable attention has been paid to changes in their biochemistry and morphology. One major concept of the ageing process is that it involves the loss of irreplaceable cells, such as the neurons. This topic has been reviewed several times but usually without critical appraisal of the data. However, there are growing doubts about whether or not there is a universal loss of neurons with ageing (HANLEY, 1974), but it is fair to say that such a loss is still 'believed'.

6.1.1 Neuronal loss

Gross observations from cross-sectional studies of the ageing brain of humans suggests that there is an overall shrinkage with age. Several studies over the last century have claimed an age-related neuron loss occurring in such diverse species as bees and man. Equally just as many studies imply that this is not the case. This argument may never be resolved for various reasons. Firstly, there are technical difficulties in sampling organs as large and as complex as the human brain. Other factors have also been ignored such as the measurement of tissue shrinkage during processing for histological examination. Secondly, experiments on animals suggest that developmental conditions (including dietary balance and sufficiency), can influence neuron number and synapse formation. If this is also true for humans then it is impossible to be certain about neuronal loss. Thirdly, research on laboratory mammals indicates that neuronal loss is not a consistent feature of ageing. Only one recent study has claimed massive neuronal loss in old animals, but the methods used involved the mechanical disruption of tissues prior to cell counting. These authors recorded losses of cells of over 50%, but took no account of the altered osmotic fragility of old cells (see section 6.2.6).

Bearing these criticisms in mind there does appear to be a disease-associated loss of neurons in some regions of the brain, for example in senile dementia and Parkinson's disease. The work that has led to this conclusion requires confirmation from other laboratories but is of obvious importance when considering the usefulness of therapeutic intervention in such disease states.

6.1.2   Age-related changes in cellular morphology

We have already discussed the age-pigment lipofuscin in the 'waste-product' theory of ageing (Chapter 4). Other morphological changes have been observed, ranging from fragmentation of the rough endoplasmic reticulum, degeneration of myofibrils in muscle tissue and extensive damage to the mitochondria. The latter can be observed in almost all old cells, and it has been argued (MIQUEL et al., 1980) that this is to do with free-radical damage to these organelles.

6.1.3   Cellular function

How can we make a functional assessment of a cell? It really depends on the type of cell under investigation. Thus, for example, one can study hormone production, protein synthesis or axonal transport, and indeed age-related changes in some of these variables have previously been discussed. A major question concerns age-related changes in stem-cell populations. We have described the fixed number of cell population doublings that take place in vitro but is this also the case in vivo? The transplantation of tissues between immunologically compatible (histocompatible), syngeneic animals (see Chapter 5) have been used to address such questions. In studies dating from the early 1960s Krohn undertook a series of transplants using ovary and skin grafts. He demonstrated that young fertilized ovaries, or eggs, functioned less well in old as compared to young recipients. Thus, factors outside the ovary affect reproductive ability in the ageing rodent (see Chapter 5). However, the results of these studies were not easy to interpret because of the variability found in the tissues of old animals.

The skin grafting results were also equivocal. In some mice the grafts from old animals grew as well as those from younger mice. During successive transplants the grafts became progressively smaller and many were lost, but this was common to samples from both young and old sources. A major problem in this study was that arising from cells from the host tissue migrating into the transplant during the process of wound repair.

In an attempt to overcome the problem of the identification of 'host-tissue', transplants of bone-marrow stem-cells have been employed. Marrow cells are easy to transplant by direct injection into the recipient's blood stream.

However, as mentioned in Chapter 5, the host has to be *lethally irradiated* to kill all of its intrinsic stem-cell population. Micklem used an abnormal chromosome to identify donor stem-cells in an elegant study of the division capacity of marrow stem-cells in mice. After 12 months in the first host the marrow cells were transplanted into a second recipient and the cells checked for the presence of the abnormal chromosome to make certain that they were from the original donor. This procedure was repeated annually and after about four successive transplants the stem-cells were found to have a reduced capacity to re-populate the host's marrow. It was therefore concluded that the maximum life-span of the mouse was very close to that of the functional division capacity of the marrow cells and that they were programmed in some way to age and die at the same time.

These experiments have been criticized for several reasons. It can be difficult to differentiate between the donor and host tissues, and successive transplantations can cause non-specific damage to the cells. Also the stem-cell pool can become 'exhausted' in conditions where constant division is stimulated. HARRISON (1978) has discussed these, and related problems, and proposed three criteria to avoid ambiguous results in transplant experiments:

(*i*) Function must be investigated, that is intrinsic ageing must be measured by a loss of *functional ability*.

(*ii*) *Identity* of the transplanted tissue must be unambiguous.

(*iii*) There must be adequate *control* built into the experimental design; young and old animal tissues should be treated in an identical fashion.

Harrison and his co-workers studied mice with a genetic defect which caused a hereditary anaemia due to stem-cell abnormalities. In this case the mice did not require prior lethal irradiation. It was shown that if the transplant was successful then the anaemia was cured. This experiment met the criteria set out above in all ways. Red-cell production could be measured in the recipients after transplantation, so a direct measure of stem-cell function was obtained. Since the cure of the hereditary anaemia *never occurred spontaneously* the donor cells were identified unambiguously. In addition, the experiments were controlled in that the effects of both young and old donor cells could be compared in the recipients. In these studies there was no evidence for intrinsic ageing of the red cell producing stem-cells.

This is an area of investigation beset with technical problems, particularly with regard to the procedure of transplantation itself. The ever-increasing sophistication of the various experiments illustrates the effect of an increase in our knowledge of the stem-cell population and the procedures which can damage them. It is only when such factors are adequately controlled that suitable experiments can be performed to study the ageing process.

6.2   Molecular biology of ageing

All organisms are comprised of complex molecules and macromolecules. In most cases the cells of a metazoan are supported by an extracellular matrix of protein macromolecules, which in the animal is mainly collagen. There have been many attempts to investigate the changes in the amounts of the chief classes of molecules found in cells and tissues, such as DNA, RNA, lipids (fats), sugars and the larger carbohydrate polymers such as glycogen, and proteins. This section will deal principally with the types of changes that take place within molecules with age, particularly DNA, proteins and lipids.

Any *system* is comprised of sub-units which act together to perform a function which cannot be perfomed by the individual components. In the discussion of the physiology of ageing we referred to the process of homeostasis by which the organism maintained a *steady-state* in the face of environmental change. Cells also maintain homeostasis through repair and turnover of their molecular structure.

All molecules undergo conformational changes with time and become disordered, perhaps owing to the effects of temperature or free-radicals. How then does an organism overcome this problem? Firstly, it may have a large excess of cells or molecules, each capable of performing the same function, this is the concept of redundancy (see Chapter 4). Secondly, it may have efficient *repair* mechanisms. Thirdly, it may be able to remove degenerate molecules and synthesize new ones, and finally, all three forms of protection may operate simultaneously. As complex molecules were evolved, maintenance and self-replication processes were also developed. Such processes have been termed 'life-extending' strategies (CUTLER, 1978). These strategies must have been very efficient because eventually these molecules evolved into the life-forms present today.

6.2.1 Changes in DNA

DNA has been considered a prime target for age-changes in all living organisms. This macromolecule is unique in that it has to replicate, and maintain itself, so that the primary genetic message (the genome) of the cell is preserved through cell division and any accidental events which may damage the DNA. In situations other than cell division DNA has to be maintained so that its function as a template for other cellular molecules is preserved for the life-span of the cell.

6.2.2 DNA damage

Various agents induce damage in DNA by either physical, chemical or biological actions. DNA can be broken, distorted or chemically altered, and the source of the agent causing this damage can be either from within the cell or some external source. Free-radicals (see Chapter 4) and other reactive metabolites of *normal* cellular metabolism, can cause 'cross-linkage' of DNA to DNA, or DNA to intranuclear proteins. Body temperature has been implicated as the cause of the loss of bases from the DNA polymer and the subsequent development of so-called 'single-strand' breaks. Other agents such as UV radiation, gamma- and X-rays all cause specific types of damage ranging from the distortion of the helix in the case of UV, and either base removal or damage from free-radicals generated by the gamma- or X-rays. Chemical mutagens and carcinogens also cause damage to DNA, as does viral DNA which can be inserted into the genome of the host and so alter the information content of the cell. It is of interest that viral DNA can be detected in cells from old animals when compared to young ones (ONO and CUTLER, 1978).

Mutations may also be a significant cause of age-related disfunction. They can arise either from errors in DNA-replication during the process of mitosis, or by the mis-pairing of bases at the site of damage in the DNA molecule, or they can be the consequence of errors in the enzymic processes responsible for the synthesis of DNA.

6.2.3 Cellular lesions generated by DNA damage

The effect of the various lesions described above depends on several factors. In general any alteration of the information content of the DNA can have substantial effects on cellular functions. For example, various physiological events follow a mutation, and the consequences rely very much on whether or not we are dealing with a homozygote or a heterozygote, and whether or not the gene affected is dominant or recessive. Most mutations are probably not lethal, especially since in a differentiated cell much of the DNA is not expressed. It is therefore highly probable that a mutation would be in a non-transcribed (repressed) region rather than a transcribed (de-repressed) one.

A mutation in a repressed zone would be 'silent', but this situation could be changed if the cell had to undergo either division or respond to a hormone, and so utilize a previously unused region of the genome. Mutations in gene-control regions could cause gene repression or de-repression which may then result in synthesis of the 'wrong molecules at the wrong time'. It has been shown, for example, that 'brain cells' from old mice contain significant quantities of RNA coding for the protein globin, whereas this has not been found in similar cells from young animals. If the mutation involves genes which control cell division, then abnormal cell proliferation may lead to tumour production, or other disease states. A mutation in the transcribed region of the DNA would be expressed immediately in terms of altered RNA and hence protein (either structural proteins or enzymes).

6.2.4 DNA repair

Several DNA repair systems have been discovered. It is possible to repair strand-breaks, remove damaged bases and insert new ones (excision repair). There is also increasing evidence that efficient repair of some forms of DNA damage is correlated with the maximum life-span potential of several mammalian species (see Chapter 4).

In differentiated post-mitotic cells certain areas of the genome cannot be transcribed owing to the presence of histone proteins. Certainly there seems to be a decreased ability for the chromatin from old animals to support some aspects of RNA synthesis – the supposed age-related reduction in chromatin template activity (see Chapter 4). The presence of age-related DNA inter-strand cross-links or DNA protein cross-links, may also hinder the repair of

DNA damage because access to the nucleic acid polymer by repair enzymes is restricted. Thus, it is possible that DNA damage could outstrip repair in such cells.

One of the predictions of the 'error catastrophe' theory of ageing is that the fidelity of DNA polymerase enzymes would be reduced in extracts from aged cells. Recently, studies using human diploid, fibroblast-like cells in tissue culture demonstrated a reduction in the fidelity of cytoplasmic DNA polymerases from senescent cells, with error frequencies between 2 and 3.4 times greater than those from enzymes prepared from young cultures. The main mispairing that seemed to take place was between guanine and thymine in these preparations. Great care must be taken in the interpretation of these results, however, because, as the authors point out (MURRAY and HOLLIDAY, 1981), the error frequency of DNA polymerase *in vitro* is much greater than when DNA is synthesized *in vivo*.

6.2.5 Proteins

Intracellular enzymes Various investigations have been made on the effects of age on the activities and concentrations of intracellular enzymes. The most frequently studied have been the enzymes involved in intermediate metabolism which have a relatively short half-life. The observations have been contradictory: in some cases enzyme activities increased with age, and in others they decreased. The changes are tissue specific and to a certain extent vary depending on the species and the strain of organism studied.

Protein structure More recently, with the stimulus of the 'error catastrophe' theory of ageing, the study of the structure of intracellular proteins has been initiated.

So-called 'error' containing proteins have been detected in cells from old animals and in senescent cells from tissue culture. However, the techniques employed have been somewhat crude. The early experimental work in this field relied on a test of the thermal stability of a population of protein molecules. It had been shown in the early 1960s that the proteins produced by certain bacterial mutants contained incorrect amino-acid insertions, and that such proteins had a *decreased thermal stability*. Using cultures of human diploid, fibroblast-like cells, and a fungus *Neurospora*, Holliday and his co-workers demonstrated a decreased thermal stability in enzymes prepared from *crude homogenates* of cultures of different ages. Similar preparations have been made from the organs of several species and other tissue culture sources over the past decade. As you may have guessed the results are contradictory. The main reason for this is that many of the studies employ different techniques and hence they are difficult to compare. A major criticism of this work is the difference between enzyme thermal stability when comparing *crude* and *pure* homogenates. There are age-related increases in the levels of lysosomal enzymes in many cells, and if they are homogenized, without due precautions being taken to remove or neutralize these enzymes, then it is possible that artefactual damage to the proteins in the homogenate will take place.

The fundamental assumption that the decreased thermal stability of proteins is due to incorrect amino-acid insertions has been questioned. Rothstein has strongly argued the case for post-translational protein changes, in other words alterations in *conformation*. He has shown that the proteins of old organisms undergo conformational changes. Part of the reason for this is the lower turnover rate of proteins in older organisms, hence, the proteins remain in the cells for longer periods prior to their destruction. Various factors, such as prolonged exposure to body temperature and perhaps free-radicals, would mean a higher probability of conformational change.

Enzyme specificity It has been argued that the enzymes involved in DNA, RNA and protein synthesis become *less specific* with age. In its simplest case this postulated error frequency could be due to a failure to discriminate between closely-related amino acids. Various investigators have attempted to force old cells to 'make mistakes' by presenting amino-acid analogues, which are sufficiently similar to naturally-occurring amino acids to be taken up during protein synthesis. Senescent cells in culture were less able to differentiate between methionine and ethionine (the analogue of the sulphur-containing amino acid methionine). A decreased ability to discriminate between such molecules has also been detected in the intact animal.

Extra-cellular proteins Collagen is one of the commonest proteins in the body, and it is the most important connective-tissue protein (HALL, 1976). Collagen is synthesized by fibroblasts as a precursor molecule, tropocollagen, which then polymerizes by means of various cross-links to form a mature collagen fibril. The tropocollagen molecules assemble both lengthwise and laterally, and the co-valent cross-links are essential for the attainment of peak physiological strength.

Age-related studies of collagen have mainly taken place on rat skin and tail tendon collagen. The latter material is very convenient in that the skin surrounding the tail can be cut and long strips of almost pure collagen removed for both physical and chemical analysis. It is possible to cause heat shrinkage of the collagen molecule. The classical experiment involves a study of the thermal contraction of collagen at 60°C. If small weights are hung on to strips of collagen then the shrinkage force generated by heating can be counteracted. Much greater weights have to be used to prevent the thermal shrinkage of 'old' collagen. Previous experiments have shown that the more heavily 'cross-linked' the protein is, the greater the thermal shrinkage, hence the claim for an increase in collagen cross-linkage with age. Other physico-chemical tests have also confirmed these observations, such as alterations in the osmotic swelling properties at a defined pH, and altered collagen extractability with age.

A study of collagen extractability in the mouse shows that collagen in other tissues such as bone, muscle and lungs, does not always behave in the same way as that of skin and tail tendon (SCHOFIELD, 1981). Thus, lung collagen had high levels of insoluble (i.e. cross-linked) collagen throughout the period investigated whereas in bone there was no increase in collagen cross-linkage after about 6 months of age (Fig. 6–1).

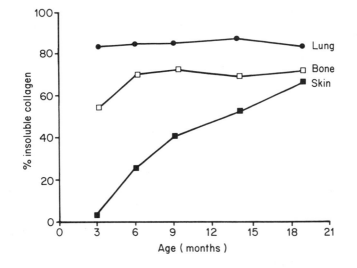

Fig. 6–1   Levels of insoluble collagen from various tissues at different stages of the lifespan (modified with permission from SCHOFIELD, 1981).

6.2.6   Lipids

As an animal ages its ability to synthesize, degrade and excrete lipid decreases. This leads to an accumulation of lipid in both blood and tissues. Various studies have reported an increase in the levels of serum triglycerides and serum cholesterol in man, monkeys and rats. Attempts to manipulate cholesterol levels by altering the saturation of the dietary fat intake have been unsuccessful. Such diets usually employ either high concentrations of animal fats such as beef lard, with a polyunsaturated : saturated fatty acid ratio of 0.2 : 1, or mixtures of safflower oil and beef lard in the ratio of 1 : 1. It has been shown that irrespective of the type of dietary lipid, the serum cholesterol increases with age. Experiments involving the use of radio-labelled cholesterol show that in older animals there is a slower turnover of cholesterol in peripheral tissues and that such changes probably contribute to the increase in serum cholesterol with advancing age.

A study of isolated fat cells has indicated an age-related decrease in the lipolytic response to various doses of adrenalin. Yet, if the sizes of the adipocytes isolated from animals of various ages are matched, then this age-related decrease is no longer apparent.

At the intracellular level, it has been shown that there is an age-related decline in the rate of synthesis of membrane phospholipids. The levels of some membrane lipids are altered with age and this can influence the activity of membrane-associated enzymes. It has been shown that the activity of the membrane transport enzyme, sodium–potassium adenosine triphosphatase increased after essential phospholipid precursors were added to the diet of aged animals. The feeding of increased levels of essential phospholipid precursors was also claimed to increase membrane fluidity in aged rat liver cell membrane.

The physico-chemical measurement of variables such as membrane fluidity have mainly been studied in red blood cells. Investigations so far indicate that there is an alteration in the lipid:protein ratio, and that these, and other cellular and membrane changes cause a decrease in membrane fluidity. These changes in the physico-chemical state of the membrane could contribute to the increased fragility of these cells to osmotic challenge.

Changes in cell lipids, particularly with regard to peroxidation and cross-linking effects with proteins, could be of paramount importance to the ageing cell. The micro-structure of the lipo-protein cell membrane could be influenced in many ways, with a considerable variety of effects on the cell itself. The changes measured so far have implicated alterations in membrane fluidity, which may in turn influence the transfer of organic molecules to and from the cell interior. Damage from free-radicals may very well lead to focal lesions which in turn could initiate an immune attack against the cell. In addition, the protein molecules that act as receptors in membranes may then be altered in some way so as to alter the quantitative binding of hormones to a particular cell.

Further Reading

General reading

BEHNKE, J. A., FINCH, C. E. and MOMENT, G. B. (eds.) (1978). *The Biology of Aging*. Plenum Press, N.Y.

BROCKLEHURST, J. C. (ed.) (1978). *Textbook of Geriatric Medicine and Gerontology*, 2nd edn. Churchill Livingstone, Edinburgh, London and N.Y.

COMFORT, A. (1979). *The Biology of Senescence*, 3rd edn. Elsevier, N.Y.

KOHN, R. R. (1971). *Principles of Mammalian Aging*. Prentice-Hall, Inc., Englewood Cliffs, New Jersey.

LAMB, M. J. (1977). *Biology of Ageing*. Blackie, Glasgow and London.

ROCKSTEIN, M. (ed.) (1974). *Theoretical Aspects of Aging*. Academic Press, Inc., N.Y., San Francisco and London.

SCHOFIELD, J. D. and DAVIES, I. (1978). Theories of Aging, in Brocklehurst, J. C. (ed.) *Textbook of Geriatric Medicine and Gerontology*, 2nd edn. Churchill Livingstone, Edinburgh, London and N.Y.

STREHLER, B. L. (1962). *Time, Cells and Aging*. Academic Press, N.Y. and London.

Specific references

BENJAMIN, B. and OVERTON, E. (19—). Prospects for mortality decline in England and Wales. *Population Trends*, **23**, 22–34.

CLARKE, J. M. and MAYNARD-SMITH, J. (1963). Two phases of ageing in Drosophila subobscura. *Journal of Experimental Biology*, **38**, 679–84.

CRISTOFALO, V. J. and STANULIS, B. M. (1978). Cell Aging: a model system approach, in Behnke, J. A. *et al.* (eds.). *The Biology of Aging*. Plenum Press, N.Y.

CURTIS, H. J. (1971). Genetic factors in aging. *Advances in Genetics*, **16**, 305–24.

CUTLER, R. G. (1978). Evolutionary biology of senescence, in Behnke, J. A. *et al.*, (eds.). *The Biology of Aging*. Plenum Press, N.Y.

DANIELLI, J. F. and MUGGLETON, A. (1959). Some alternative states of amoeba, with special reference to life-span. *Gerontologia*, **3**, 76–90.

DAVIES, I. and FOTHERINGHAM, A. P. (1981). Lipofuscin – Does it affect cellular performance? *Experimental Gerontology*, **16**, 119–25.

DAVIES, I. and FOTHERINGHAM, A. P. (1981a). The influence of age on the response of the supraoptic nucleus of the hypothalamo-neurohypophyseal system to physiological stress. II. Quantitative morphology. *Mechanisms of Ageing and Development*, **15**, 367–78.

EDNEY, E. B. and GILL, R. W. (1968). Evolution of senescence and specific longevity. *Nature (Lond.)*, **220**, 281–2.

FINCH, C. E., JONEC, V., WISNER, J. R., SINHA, Y. N., DEVELLIS, J. S. and SWERDLOFF, R. S. (1977). Hormone production by pituitary and testes of male C57BL/6J mice during aging. *Endocrinology*, **101**, 1310–17.

GUSSECK, D. J. (1974). Endocrine mechanisms and aging. *Advances in Gerontological Research*, **4**, 105–66.

GUTHRIE, R. D. (1969). Senescence as an adaptive trait. *Perspectives in Biological Medicine*, **12**, 313–24.

HALL, D. A. (1976). *Ageing of Connective Tissue*. Academic Press, London.

HALLIWELL, B. (1981). Free radicals, oxygen toxicity, and aging, in Sohal, R. S. (ed.) *Age Pigments*. Elsevier/North-Holland Biomedical Press, Amsterdam, N.Y. and Oxford.

HANLEY, T. (1974). Neuronal 'fall-out' in the aging brain; a critical review of the quantitative data. *Age and Ageing*, **3**, 133–51.

HARMAN, D. (1956). Aging: a theory based on free radical and radiation chemistry. *Journal of Gerontology*, **11**, 298–300.

HARMAN, S. M. and TSITOURAS, P. D. (1980). Reproductive hormones in aging men. 1. Measurement of sex steroids, basal luteinizing hormone, and Leydig cell response to human chorionic gonadotropin. *Journal of Clinical Endocrinology and Metabolism*, **51**, 35–40.

HARRISON, D. E. (1978). Is limited cell proliferation the clock that times aging? in Behnke, J. A. *et al.*, (eds.). *The Biology of Aging*. Plenum Press, N.Y.

HART, R. W. and SETLOW, R. B. (1974). Correlation between deoxyribonucleic acid excision repair and life-span in a number of mammalian species. *Proceedings of National Academy of Science (USA)*, **71**, 2169–73.

HAYFLICK, L. (1965). The limited *in vitro* lifetime of human diploid cell strains. *Experimental Cell Research*, **37**, 614–36.

HAYFLICK, L. and MOOREHEAD, P. S. (1961). The serial cultivation of human diploid cell strains. *Experimental Cell Research*, **25**, 585–621.

KAY, M. M. B. and MAKINODAN, T. (1981). Relationship between aging and the immune system. *Progress in Allergy*, **29**, 134–81.

KOHN, R. R. (1963). Human aging and disease. *Journal of Chronic Diseases*, **16**, 5–35.

LANSING, A. I. (1959). General biology of senescence, in Birren, J. E. (ed.). *Handbook of aging and the individual: Psychological and Biological Aspects*. University of Chicago Press, Chicago.

LEOPOLD, A. C. (1978). The biological significance of death in plants, in Behnke, J. A. *et al.*, (eds.). *The Biology of Aging*. Plenum Press, N.Y.

MARTIN, G. M. (1978). Genetic syndromes in man with potential relevance to the pathobiology of aging, in Bergsma, D. and Harrison, D. E. (eds.). *Genetic Effects on Aging*. Alan R. Liss, Inc., N.Y.

MEDAWAR, P. B. (1952). *An Unsolved Problem in Biology*. Lewis, London.

MERTZ, D. B. (1975). Senescent decline in flour beetle strains selected for early adult fitness. *Physiological Zoology*, **48**, 1–23.

MIQUEL, J., ECONOMOS, A. C., FLEMING, J. and JOHNSON, J. E., Jr. (1980). Mitochondrial role in cell aging. *Experimental Gerontology*, **15**, 575–91.

MURRAY, V. and HOLLIDAY, R. (1981). Increased error frequency of DNA-polymerases from senescent human-fibroblasts. *Journal of Molecular Biology*, **146**, 55–76.

NELSON, J. F., LATHAM, K. R. and FINCH, C. E. (1975). Plasma testosterone levels in C57BL/6J male mice: effects of age and disease. *Acta Endocrinologica*, **80**, 744–53.

ONO, T. and CUTLER, R. G. (1978). Age-dependent relaxation of gene repression: increase of endogenous leukemia virus-related and globin-related RNA in brain and liver of mice. *Proceedings of National Academy of Science (USA)*, **75**, 4431–5.

ORGEL, L. E. (1970). The maintenance of the accuracy of protein synthesis and its relevance to ageing: a correction. *Proceedings of National Academy of Science (USA)*, **67**, 1476–9.

ROTH, G. S. (1978). Altered biochemical responsiveness and hormone receptors during aging, in Behnke, J. A. *et al.*, (eds.). *The Biology of Aging*. Plenum Press, N.Y.

SACHER, G. A. (1959). Relation of life-span to brain weight and body weight in mammals, in Wolstenholme, G. E. W. and O'Connor, M. (eds.). *Ciba Foundation Colloquia on Ageing*, **5**, 115–33. Churchill, London.

SCHOFIELD, J. D. (1981). Connective tissue ageing: differences between mouse tissues in age-related changes in collagen extractability. *Experimental Gerontology*, **15**, 113–20.

SHARMA, H. K. and ROTHSTEIN, M. (1980). Altered enolase in aged *Turbatrix aceti* results from conformational changes in the enzyme. *Proceedings of National Academy of Science (USA)*, **77**, 5865–8.

SHOCK, N. (1956). Some physiological aspects of ageing in man. *Bulletin New York Academy of Medicine*, **32**, 268–83.

SOHAL, R. S. (ed.) (1981). *Age Pigments*. Elsevier/North-Holland Biomedical Press, Amsterdam, New York and Oxford.

SOKAL, R. R. (1970). Senescence and genetic load: evidence from *Tribolium Science (Wash.)*, **167**, 1733–4.

SONNEBORN, T. M. (1978). The origin, evolution, nature, and causes of aging, in Behnke, J. A. *et al.*, (eds.). *The Biology of Aging*. Plenum Press, N.Y.

ROSE, M. and CHARLESWORTH, B. (1980). A test of evolutionary theories of senescence. *Nature (Lond.)*, **287**, 141–3.

ROSS, M. H., LUSTBADER, E. and BRAS, G. (1976). Dietary practices and growth responses as predictors of longevity. *Nature (Lond.)*, **262**, 548–53.

WALFORD, R. L. (1969). *The Immunologic Theory of Aging*. Munksgaard, Copenhagen.

WILLIAMS, G. C. (1957). Pleiotropy, natural selection, and the evolution of senescence. *Evolution*, **11**, 398–411.

WOOLHOUSE, H. W. (1978). Cellular and metabolic aspects of senescence in higher plants, in Behnke, J.A. *et al.*, (eds.). *The Biology of Aging*. Plenum Press, N.Y.

Index